Single Crochet **for Beginners**

Cindy Crandall-Frazier

©2005 Cindy Crandall-Frazier

Published by

kp **kp books**
An Imprint of F+W Publications

700 East State Street • Iola, WI 54990-0001
715-445-2214 • 888-457-2873

Our toll-free number to place an order or obtain a free catalog is 800-258-0929.

Lily® Sugar'n Cream, Red Heart®, TLC®, Coats and Clark, Inc.©,
DMC®, Caron®, Lion Brand®, Wool-Ease®, Patons®

Library of Congress Catalog Number: 2005924836

ISBN: 0-89689-176-3

Edited by Candy Wiza
Designed by Marilyn McGrane

Printed in China

Dedication

For Toddy,

who first taught me

how to crochet.

Table of Contents

Do you love the feel
of soft, squishy skeins
of yarn? Do you yearn
to buy beautiful colors
and take them home
to turn into something
fun or useful? Do you
know someone who
seems so content to
crochet that they never
put down their hook
for long? If you said
yes to any of these
questions, then pick up
this book and let's get
started.

Introduction

Crochet is accomplished by pulling loops of yarn, string or thread through other loops with a simple hook. When you crochet, you create the fabric of an item at the same time you create the item itself. Using this idea of connected loops, people have designed fine laces, warm items like mittens, hats and sweaters, and even hard, useful items like baskets.

The craft of crochet is unique. Mistakes are easy to correct. You just pull out loops until you have pulled out your mistake, then pick up one loop and rework. Crochet is easy to measure as you go along because you can take your hook out and lay your fabric against whoever or whatever you are fitting. Crochet is a wonderful medium in which to express your own creativity after you learn the basics.

Single crochet is just one stitch used in the craft of crochet. It is the short-est, simplest stitch for making a cro-cheted fabric. Single crochet produces stitches that are short and close to-gether, therefore the fabric can be both sturdy and snug. "Single Crochet for Beginners" will teach you how to make the basic fabric and its variations, then go on to show you how to shape that fabric, all the while creating playful and practical items. With the techniques in this book, you will be able to design many projects of your own.

Your materials are very portable and you can crochet while doing other things. A hook and a ball of yarn can go along with you on a hike, to gather-ings with friends or on a car trip. You can crochet while talking, watching TV or listening to your favorite music. You also can put your crochet in a shoulder bag and crochet while you walk (in a safe place of course).

Be patient with yourself while you are learning. As with every new skill, you will improve each time you pick up your hook and yarn. If you need help, ask friends or relatives who crochet, or ask for help at your local yarn store. Your public library may have an instructional video. On the Web you can view short videos teaching many of the crochet stitches at http://www.stitchguide.com.

Imagine being able to make toys, warm items for yourself and friends and baby gifts for the new baby in your fam-ily or neighborhood. Choosing beautiful colors and textures of yarn can be as much fun as choosing from a big box of crayons. Now, imagine yourself sitting in front of a cozy fireplace with your crochet work after sledding or on a balcony at the beach in summer. Cro-cheting can be a relaxing and satisfying activity almost anytime and anyplace. No wonder some people can't seem to put their hooks down!

How to Use This Book

It is important to read the information about yarn and yarn tools in the first chapter. Then learn the basic crochet stitch in the second chapter. Every project after that has a purpose, whether it is to provide practice, teach you something new or challenge you to make something larger or more complex. You don't have to make every project to learn lots of new skills. The projects at the beginning of each chapter are the easiest ones for that chapter.

Take the time to become friends with a project or a new skill before you move on. Chapter 2 provides several ways to practice your basic skills and make sure your stitch count remains the same as your row count grows. Chapter 3 offers more practice with simple squares and rectangles while showing you different ways to use color. Chapter 4 teaches the back and front loop variations. Each of these stitches make a fabric with a different look and feel. In Chapter 5 you will learn how to increase and decrease. The bow tie is a short project to introduce these skills, the scarf a longer one. There is a project for decreasing in a pattern to create a round ending for hats and a way to increase and decrease at right angles to make a box. Working in the round is the subject of Chapter 6 with two ways to make tube shapes and one way to make a flat round. The baby sweater, mittens, hat and vest in the last chapter employ a number of skills in each project and require you to pay more attention to the pattern. Check the skills list before you start a project. Don't forget to give yourself a great big pat on the back each time you learn something new.

Chapter 1

Meet your materials and get to know their different personalities. How do they interact with each other? You can start making finger chains

Chain Loops

with just about any string or yarn you find around the house. Or, make them from yarns with a variety of colors and textures that you purchased at the store. Learn how to hold the yarn and a hook. When you can use the hook to make your chains, you are really starting to crochet! There is a lot of important information in Chapter 1. The techniques will get you off to a good start. You can refer to this information as you branch out and try new projects and start to make designs of your own.

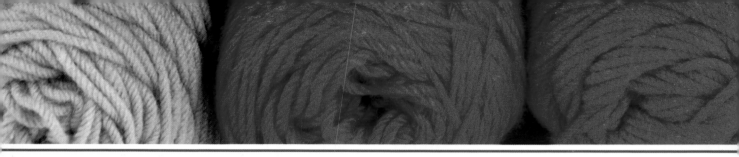

Yarns

Wool, silk and angora yarn.

Fibers for yarns come from both natural and synthetic sources. There also are many combinations of fibers called "blends." The best fiber for crocheting warm items is wool. Wool is sheared from the backs of sheep in the spring when they don't need it. Items made from wool used to require hand washing so they wouldn't shrink or fall apart. Now, wool comes in machine-washable forms, either blended with synthetics or treated to resist shrinking. Cotton is another popular natural fiber. Both 100 percent cotton yarns and yarns made of cotton blended with acrylic are available. One hundred percent acrylic yarns are often the least expensive and easiest to find.

Most people choose their yarn because they like the color. Quality is important too. Run your hand over the surface of the skein. Do you like the way it feels? Stretch several inches of yarn. Does it give a little and then pull back when released? Elasticity (stretchiness) may be important for your project. Pinch a strand between your thumb and forefinger. Does it squash down or does it feel hard under your fingers? Dense, hard yarn might work well for a bag or a rug, but loft* is best for sweaters, hats and mittens.

Learning to crochet will be easier with yarns that have a relatively smooth finish. Fuzzy, hairy and loopy yarns are best saved for when you have more experience. Also, it is easier to see your stitches if your yarn is smooth and not too dark.

Note: Loft is the thickness or fluffiness of a yarn. It enables the fibers it is made of to fill the spaces between the stitches in fiber crafts, such as knitting and crochet.

How Yarn is Sold

After yarn is spun, it is wound into skeins of many different shapes and sizes. Just for fun, the next time you visit a yarn store, take note of how different yarns are wound and packaged.

Usually you can start to crochet immediately using a yarn end on the outside of the skein or an end that is tucked inside. Look for instructions on your label. Sometimes yarn is sold in a hank that will get tangled if you don't wind it into a ball. Undo the large loop of a hank and place it around the back of a chair, or have someone hold it with both hands inside the loop. See page 40 for instructions for winding a ball.

Hank of yarn.

Washing

 Do not wash

 Hand wash in warm water

 Hand wash at stated temperature

 Machine wash

 Do not tumble dry

 Tumble drying OK

 Dry flat

 No bleach

 Chlorine bleach OK

Pressing

 Do not iron

 Cool iron

 Warm iron

 Hot Iron

Dry Cleaning Symbols

 Do not dry clean

 Dry cleanable in all solvents

 Dry cleanable with fluorocarbon or petroleum-based solvents only

 Dry cleanable with perchlorethylene, hydrocarbons, or a petroleum-based solvent

Ball of crochet thread.

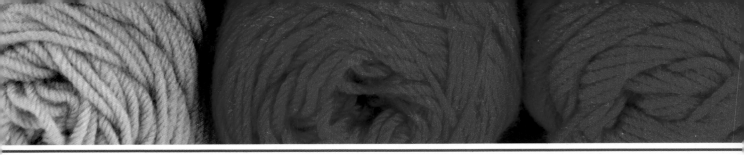

Yarn Labels

Keep your label. You may want to refer to it again. You should always try to buy enough skeins of the same dye lot when you make your first purchase. If you do need more yarn to finish your project, you will need to know the dye lot number to get a perfect match. You also may want to refer to the washing instructions (see page 13). It is a good idea to tuck a yarn label into a crocheted gift so the recipient can wash your present the correct way.

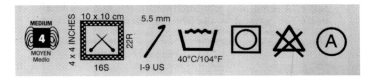

Play a game with yourself and see if you can find every item below on your yarn label.

1. Brand name of yarn.
2. Company name.
3. Fiber content (wool, cotton, acrylic, etc.).
4. Weight of the skein.
5. How many yards of yarn.
6. Thickness of the yarn (bulky, worsted, sport).
7. Color name and dye lot.
8. Washing instructions.

Make a Slip Knot

Making a slip knot is the very first step in crocheting. You also will need to make a slip knot to start your finger chains.

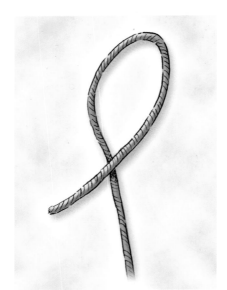

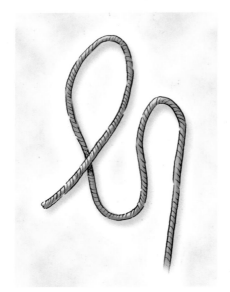

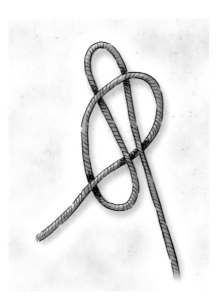

1. Make a loop with the short end of the yarn crossed over the long end.

2. Make a bend in the long end of the yarn below the loop.

3. Push the bend through the first loop from front to back.

4. Pull up on the new loop with one hand while pulling down on both the short and long ends of the yarn. You can tighten the loop by pulling the long end of the yarn.

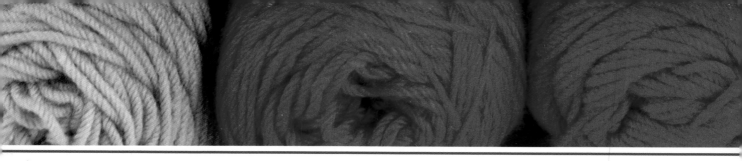

A Faster Way to Make a Slip Knot and a Verse to Remember It

Over duck's beak,

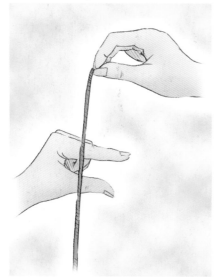

Make a duck's beak with your hand.

With the other hand take the end of the yarn.

Bring the yarn over your pincer fingers.

Under his chin,

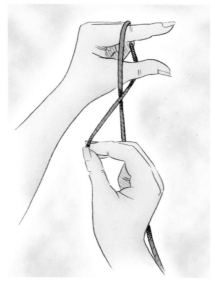

Continue to bring the yarn under your pincer fingers.

Over his beak again.

Bring the yarn over your pincer fingers again and hold it there.

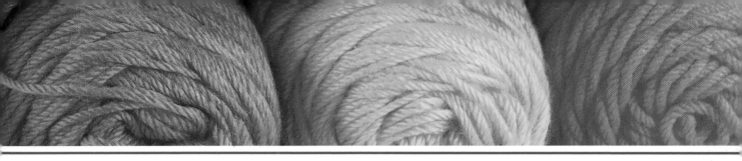

Duck tails up.

Without dropping the yarn in your other hand, point your pincer fingers down.

Grab some food.

Grab the long end of the yarn

Yum!

Pull the long end of the yarn up through the yarn that is wound around your pincer fingers.

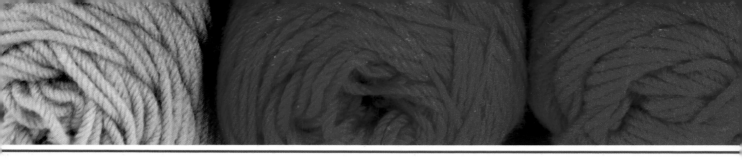

Finger Chains

Yarn and your fingers are all you need for this activity. Finger chains make fine gift ribbons, hair ties, belts and ropes. Try using different kinds of yarn and string, using multiple strands for color and thickness.

After you have made a slip knot, pick up the long end of the yarn, pulling it through each loop and tightening. If you insert your fingers in the front of each loop, the front of the chain will be facing you.

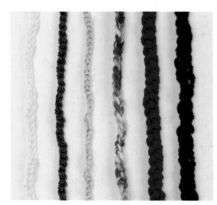

Finger chains made with various yarns.

1. Insert your thumb and index finger through the loop from the front.

3. Hold the short end with your other hand and pull the new loop up through the previous one.

2. Pick up the long end of the yarn, pinching it between the thumb and index finger.

4. Repeat Steps 1 through 3, starting in the new loop each time.

Note: *The loops may get longer as you work. You can tighten each chain as you go along to make a pretty cord.*

Finger chains make
cute little hair ribbons.

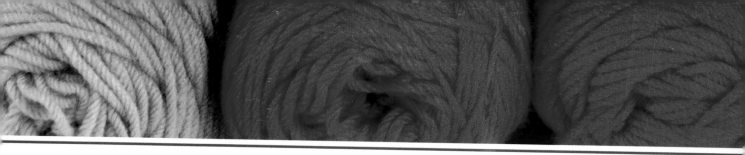

Hooks

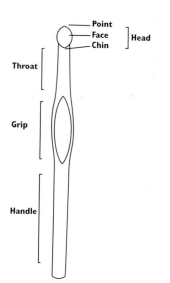

Point
Face
Chin] Head

Throat

Grip

Handle

Different brands of hooks have different personalities. The most common difference in hooks is the throat. There are hooks with narrow throats and hooks with wide throats. You get a different effect with each. Look at the hook with its face turned toward you. On a narrow hook, the throat and head are narrower than the handle. On a wide hook, the throat will be as wide as, or "in line with" the handle. Because of this, hooks with a wide throat are often called "in-line hooks." All of the projects in the first chapter call for a size H/8 (5.00 mm) hook. While you are learning, it is a good idea to have one of each kind of hook on hand, then use the one that is most comfortable for you. In later chapters, the instructions may suggest one kind of hook over another. After you gain some skill, you may want to experiment with hooks other than the most common varieties. Some are shorter than others; some have more pointed heads and some

more rounded chins. I am sure you will find that you have favorites.

You will notice a difference in the way the yarn slides along hooks made of different materials and surfaces. Aluminum hooks come in a variety of surfaces and can be found at both craft stores and yarn shops. Wood and bamboo hooks are usually found in stores that sell yarn specifically. Another source for hooks, made from bone and brass and other unusual materials, is on the Web at http://www.jklneedles.com. Check other sources on the Web too. Plastic hooks can be colorful and you may want to purchase some for fun, but they can break. The yarn may not slide as smoothly on a plastic hook as with other types of hooks. If you want to make crocheted lace with fine threads, there is another type of hook called a steel hook. A steel hook is very narrow and more standardized than a yarn hook.

Aluminum Crochet Hooks

Size 2/B (2.25 mm)

Size 3/C (2.75 mm)

Size 4/D (3.25 mm)

Size 5/E (3.50 mm)

Size 6/F (3.75 mm)

Size 7/G (4.25 mm)

Size 8/H (5.00 mm)

Size 9/I (5.50 mm)

Size 10/J (6.00 mm)

Size 10.5/K (6.50 mm)

Size 11/N (9.00 mm)

Steel Crochet Hooks

Size 14 (.75 mm)

Size 12 (1.00 mm)

Size 11 (1.10 mm)

Size 10 (1.30 mm)

Size 9 (1.40 mm)

Size 8 (1.50 mm)

Size 7 (1.65 mm)

Size 6 (1.80 mm)

Size 5 (1.90 mm)

Size 4 (2.00 mm)

Size 3 (2.10 mm)

Size 2 (2.25 mm)

Size 1 (2.75 mm)

Size 0 (3.25 mm)

Size 00 (3.50 mm)

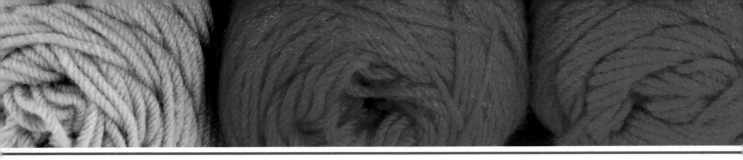

Holding the Hook and Yarn

The Hook

You can hold your hook in either the pencil position or the knife position. Use whichever is more comfortable for you.

1. The pencil position.

2. The knife position.

The Yarn

Make your slip knot. Put the hook through the loop so the short end of the yarn is toward you. Pull up the yarn around the hook. Tighten the knot next to the hook so you won't mistake it for a stitch later.

1. Drape the long end of the yarn over your pinky, ring and middle fingers on the inside of your hand.

2. Take the yarn behind your index finger, over it and toward you.

3. Close your two lower fingers gently over your yarn.

4. With your thumb and middle finger, grasp the slip knot to keep it from twisting as you work.

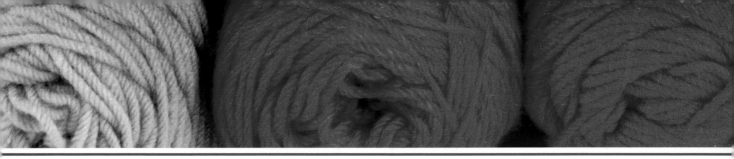

Tension

Stitch gauge ruler.

Notice how you can squeeze the yarn lightly as it flows between your middle and pointer fingers. This provides tension. Experiment with more or less tension. Remember to relax to prevent the tension from getting too tight.

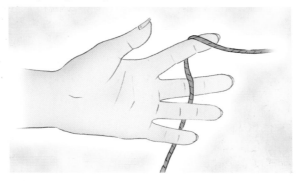

If your yarn flows too freely, wind it in and out of another couple of fingers . . .

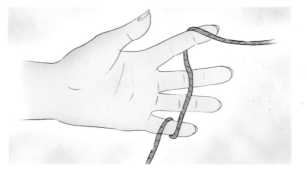

or wrap the yarn around your pinky.

Yarn and Hook Together

Crochet can be used to make a stiff fabric for sturdy items like baby footwear or baskets. Crochet also can be employed to make a supple* fabric to create sweaters, scarves and soft blankets. The trick is to use the correct hook and yarn together. Listed below are suggested hook sizes to go with the most common yarn weights.

Yarn	Stiff Fabric Hook Size	Firm Fabric	Supple Fabric
Sport Weight	D/3 (3.25 mm)	F/5 (3.75 mm)	H/8 (5.00 mm)
Double Knitting or DK	E/4 (3.50 mm)	G/6 (4.25 mm)	I/9 (5.50 mm)
Worsted Weight	F/5 (3.75 mm)	H/8 (5.00 mm)	J/10 (6.00 mm)
Bulky Weight	G/6 (4.25 mm)	I/9 (5.50 mm)	K/10½ (6.50 mm)

These are only guidelines. The brand of yarn and the fibers in your yarn will change the fabric you make. The tension applied to your work will vary the result. The brand of hook also can change the effect. Hooks with narrow throats can increase the stiffness in a project and a hook with a wide throat can increase the suppleness, for a softer fabric. Sometimes a hook with a wide throat can help if you want a stiff fabric and your yarn or thread is hard, as in the CD Box project. Experiment! Make a series of samples. Choose a yarn and work small squares; increase the size of the hook for each square. For this experiment to work well, use the same brand of hook each time.

Supple means bending or folding easily.

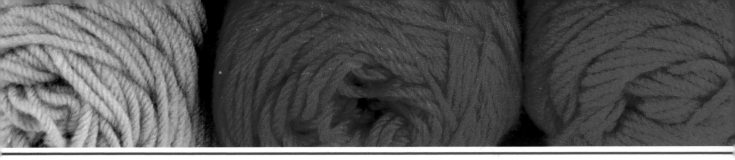

Making a Chain With the Hook

All crochet work starts from a foundation of chains. Using a hook makes this process go quickly and smoothly. Hold your hook and yarn as shown in the following instructions.

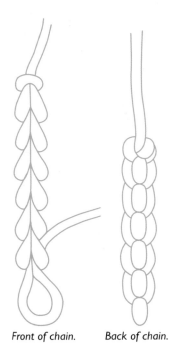

Front of chain.   *Back of chain.*

1. Keep the face of the hook toward you and the hook in front of the yarn supply. Point the hook under the yarn and then up slightly behind the yarn to catch it under the chin of the hook. This is called a yarn over.

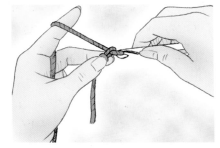

2. Turn the face of the hook down slightly and pull the yarn through the loop on the hook. This is usually expressed as "pull through" or "pull up a loop." You may want to lift the handle of the hook slightly so the chin of your hook will pass smoothly.

3. Continue to make chain stitches by repeating Steps 1 and 2 until your chain is the desired length. As you become more comfortable with holding the hook and yarn, swing the yarn over the hook with your finger that carries the yarn supply instead of making your "hook hand" do all the work.

Other Tools

Scissors: You will need a multi-purpose scissors for cutting cardboard and a pair of sharp scissors for cutting yarn. A pair of small needlework scissors works great for take-along projects.

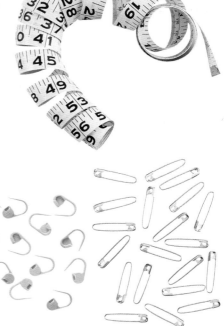

Yarn needles: Yarn needles also are called tapestry needles. They have large eyes for threading the yarn and rounded points that won't split the yarn fibers. Yarn needles are used for threading in ends and for sewing seams. A size 16 yarn needle will work for most of the projects in this book. The Vest and the CD Box require a size 13 needle.

Measuring tape: For some projects a ruler or a yardstick will do, but a measuring tape is a great tool to have in your bag. It will take long, short, straight and curved measurements and takes up very little space.

Stitch markers: These are usually found wherever yarns are sold. There are many varieties. They can look like a safety pin without the circle at the small end, or like a plastic circle that isn't completely closed. It is a good idea to have a small package of stitch markers, but if you don't, partly unbend paper clips for that purpose, or thread a small length of yarn through a stitch as a marker.

Chapter 2

Here it comes — Single Crochet! I remember the day my friend showed me how to make my first square of single crochet. I was excited because I thought I could make so many things with just that one

Lots More Loops

stitch. This book is the outgrowth of that delicious thought. I still believe today there is a lot to explore with this simple stitch. In this chapter you'll learn how to make it. Then, there are some finishing skills and several easy and playful projects to make. I have used the 4 by 4 project to teach single crochet when I have a large group of students and only a short amount of time to share the skill. After you become proficient, you may want to teach others how to make it. Try the beanbag and the 10" traditional Yarn Kid with hat and scarf. I've also included an easy way to make pompoms and tassels. Decorate!

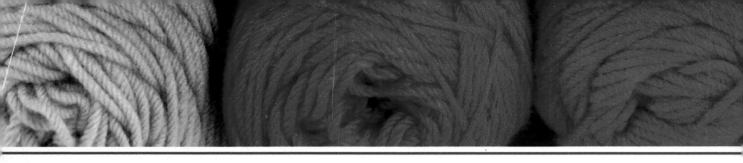

Single Crochet

The single crochet stitch is the shortest, easiest and most practical crochet stitch. With this stitch and its variations, you can create many items, including things to keep you warm.

Row One

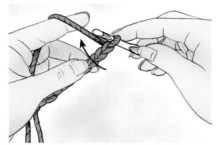

1. With the front of the chain facing you, skip the 2 chains next to the hook and insert the hook into the third chain. (The easiest place to insert the hook is in the upper part of the loop.)

2. Yarn over.

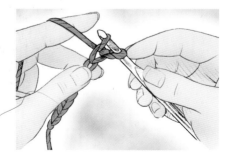

3. Pull through. There are now 2 loops on the hook.

4. Yarn over again without inserting your hook into the chain.

5. Pull through both loops. You have just made one single crochet!

Insert the hook in the next chain to the left and repeat Steps 2 through 5. You have made 2 single crochet stitches. While you are learning, place a marker on the first stitch so you will recognize it when you finish Row 2. Continue working to the left, making a single crochet in each chain stitch. If you cannot tell where the next chain is, try gently tugging on your last single crochet stitch. You will see more clearly where the last chain and the next chain are located.

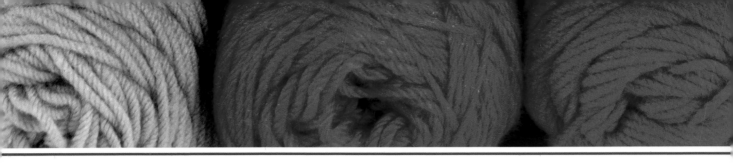

Counting Stitches

If you accidentally skip stitches, your work will become narrower. If you make extra stitches, it will become wider. To prevent either of these things from happening unintentionally, stop regularly and count the number of stitches in your row. This is very important at the beginning when you are still learning and when you start making more challenging projects. I count stitches by counting the chains along the top of a row. Count stitches before you chain one at the start of a new row. This will prevent counting the chain as a stitch and counting too many stitches.

Row Two

After you have completed the last single crochet in the last chain, continue according to the following instructions.

1. Turn your work toward you and to your left.

2. Yarn over.

3. Pull through the loop on your hook. Instructions will simply say "chain 1."

4. Find the tops of your first row of stitches. They will look just like the front of a chain. You may have to twist them toward you to see them.

5. Skip the chain you just made that is next to the hook and insert the hook under both loops of the top of the next single crochet. Complete the stitch.

Make each new row as you did in Row 2. Turn, chain 1, skip the chain and single crochet in each stitch across the row.

Note

Crochet is usually taught by skipping only one chain before you make the first single crochet in the chain row. Skipping two chains makes it easier to identify the first stitch of a row when you work back across. It also makes it easier to insert the hook for the last stitch of the second row.

Another Note

The simple "turning chain method" is used in this book. Every single crochet is made in a single crochet in the row below it. Other crochet patterns may count the chain as a stitch.

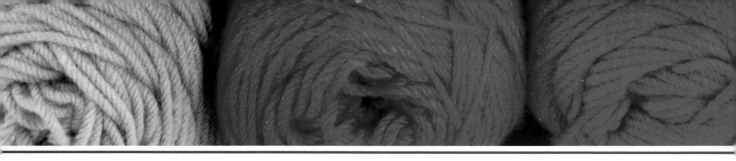

4 by 4

A 4 by 4 is a very small crochet project. It is 4 stitches wide and 4 rows long. When your 4 by 4 is completed, you can save it and use it as a button on a bag, or make a number of colorful 4 by 4s to sew on a plain hat or scarf for decoration.

Chain 6.

Row 1: Skip 2 chains and make a single crochet in the third chain from the hook. Single crochet in each of the next three chains (4 single crochets). Turn.

Row 2: Chain 1, single crochet in each of the 4 single crochets of the row below. Turn.

Row 3: Work as for row 2.

Row 4: Chain 1, single crochet across. End off and weave in the ends.

End Off

When you have completed the piece you are working on, cut it free from your yarn supply. Leave a tail long enough for weaving in or sewing a seam. Pull the last loop all the way through the last stitch. This will prevent your stitches from coming undone.

Materials

- 1 ½ yd. (2 m) worsted weight yarn
- Size H/8 (5.00 mm) crochet hook
- Scissors
- Yarn needle

Skills

- Make a chain

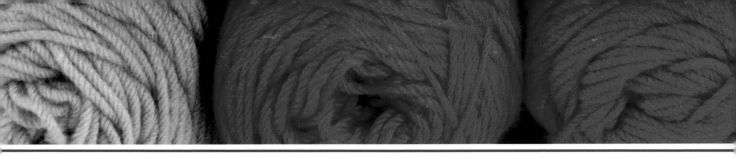

Thread the Needle

1. Hold the yarn between your thumb and forefinger and about 2" (5.0 cm) back from the end.

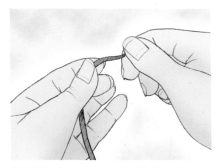

2. With the other hand, tightly twist the yarn end in the same direction it is spun.

3. Without losing twist, double the short end back, and hold it between your thumb and forefinger.

4. Pick up your needle and press the opening of the eye against your loop. Move your needle up and down a bit while pressing.

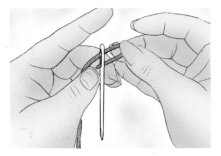

5. Pull the loop through the eye of your needle.

Weave in the Ends

Weave the end across a row.

1. Thread a needle with your yarn end.

2. With the wrong side of your work facing you, push the needle under the top strands of 5 or 6 stitches. Weave the end across a row or up and down across several rows. If you change direction, and take the needle through several more stitches, your end will be more secure.

3. Trim the remaining yarn.

Weave the end up and down across several rows.

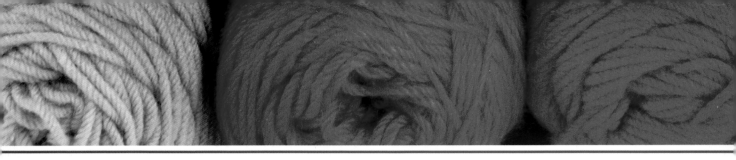

Turnover Beanbag

Named after a pastry that is usually filled with fruit, these versatile toys consist of one crocheted square filled with dry beans. When your beanbag is finished, try tossing it into the air and see how many times you can clap before you catch it.

Make a chain that is 4½" (11.25 cm) long without being stretched. Add 2 more chains.

Row 1: Skip 2 chains and single crochet in the third chain from the hook. Single crochet in each remaining chain. Turn.

Row 2: Chain 1, single crochet across. Turn.

Repeat Row 2 until your piece is as long as it is wide. You should be able to fold it diagonally and make a perfect triangle.

End off, leaving about 24" (60 cm) of yarn for sewing.

Finishing

Thread the ending length of yarn in a yarn needle. Using an overcast stitch (see page 41) sew the first open side closed, then sew the second side, leaving a 2" (5.1 cm) opening to insert the beans. Use the chain row stitches on one side and the ending row stitches as guides for your stitches, one overcast stitch in each. Fill with beans and finish sewing closed. Thread the remaining end in and cut the thread.

Sew one side of the beanbag using the ending row stitches as a guide.

Materials

- 20 yd. (19 m) worsted weight yarn
- Size H/8 (5.00 mm) crochet hook
- Ruler or measuring tape
- Scissors
- Yarn needle
- Bag of dried beans (baby limas are a good choice)

Skills

- Make a chain
- Plain single crochet
- Sew a seam

Finished size:

- 6½" (16.25 cm) × 3½" (8.75 cm)

Here are some other ideas for playing with your beanbag:

❋ Play toss n' catch with a friend, taking a step backward after a couple throws. See how far apart you can get.

❋ Place a box or basket on the floor for a target. You can make a more complicated target with masking tape on a large piece of fabric.

❋ Have a race. Everyone has to hold a beanbag between his or her ankles.

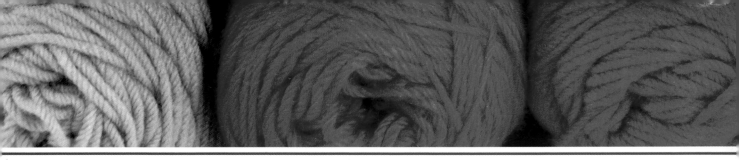

Wind a Ball of Yarn

Yarn is sold in many forms, some easier to work with than others. Check for instructions on your yarn label. If you find your skein difficult to work with, you may want to make a ball of yarn. A ball will roll easily with a light tug and make your work go more smoothly.

Overcast Stitch

1. Bring the needle behind the edge and push it through to the top side that is facing you.

2. Pull the thread all the way up.

3. Return the needle to the first position below the edge, but a short distance ahead of the first stitch.

1. Wrap yarn loosely around your first three fingers until it is thick. Always wind loosely to prevent pulling the elasticity out of your yarn.

2. Remove this yarn from your fingers, make a quarter turn, and wind some more. I like to place it on my thumb and turn it as I wind.

3. Make close diagonal winds all around your yarn. It will start to look like a ball.

Yarn that is sold in a hank will always need to be wound into a ball to keep it from tangling. To work with a hank, pull one twisted end out of the other, gently untwist it and place the resulting loop over the back of a chair. Undo the knots that hold it together and then wind it using the instructions above.

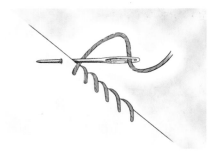

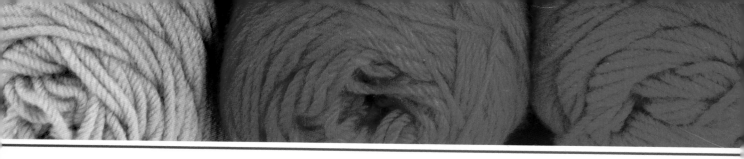

A Yarn Kid

Yarn dolls are a folk-art form related to tassels, and, like tassels, may have been around for thousands of years. Woven Mexican belts are often finished by tying the ends to look like tassel dolls. The "Yarn Kid" that results from these instructions is about 10" tall and a perfect figure for which to make small crocheted items.

1. Wind a ball of yarn that measures 7½" (18.75 cm) around. See page 40 for how to wind a ball. This will be the inner head. Set it aside.

2. To make the body, wind yarn along the 11" (27.5 cm) length of your cardboard. It will take about 160 wraps within a 3" (7.5 cm) width of the cardboard.

3. Cut a piece of yarn 12" (30.5 cm) long. Tie it tightly around the loops at one end of the cardboard. Cut through the loops at the other end and remove the cardboard.

4. Insert the head ball under the knot. Smooth the yarn over the head ball. Make sure the cut ends are even. Tie a 12" (30.5 cm) piece of yarn around the base of the head to form the neck. Set the body aside.

Materials

- 240 yd. (219 m) worsted weight yarn (I used a 5 oz. skein and had yarn left over.)
  Note: You must start with a new skein for each yarn kid.
- 8½" (21.25 cm) x 11" (27.5 cm) heavy piece of cardboard or mat board
- Scissors
- 7½" (18.75 cm) piece of string or measuring tape to measure the head

Finished Size:

- 10" tall

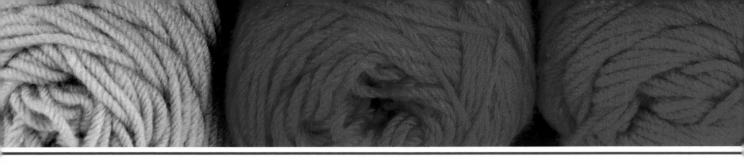

A Yarn Kid

5. Wind the yarn around the 8½" (21.25 cm) side of the cardboard. You will need about 60 wraps. This forms the arms.

6. Cut 2 pieces of yarn and tie the loops together at each end. Slide the yarn off the cardboard.

7. Tie a piece of yarn tightly around each end and approx. 1" (2.5 cm) back from the first knots. Cut the first knots.

8. Cut the loops at each end and trim as you would a pompom.

9. Decide where the front of the head will be. Split the yarn so one half is in front and one half is in back. Place the arms in the split and tie a piece of yarn under the arms to form a waist.

10. Split the rest of the loose body yarn for legs. Tie short pieces of yarn tightly around the legs approx. 1" (2.5 cm) from the bottom, allowing enough length for trimming. Cut the loops and trim.

A Yarn Kid Hat and Scarf

Dress up your yarn kid in a great hat that starts out as a simple rectangle. Choose from a variety of ways to sew the top closed. Add your choice of pompoms, tassels or ties. Or, have your Yarn Kid sport an especially colorful scarf to match or contrast with the hat.

Yarn Kid Scarf

Chain 6.

Row 1: Skip 2 chains and single crochet in the third chain from the hook. Single crochet in the remaining 3 chains. Turn.

Row 2: Chain 1, single crochet across the 4 stitches. Turn.

Repeat Row 2 until your scarf is approx. 18" (45 cm) long. End off and thread in the ends.

Materials for scarf

- 20 yd. (19 m) worsted weight yarn
- Size H/8 (5.00 mm) crochet hook
- Scissors
- Yarn needle

Skills

- Make a chain
- Plain single crochet

Finished size of scarf:

- 1" (5.5 cm) × 17" (42.5 cm)

Materials for hat

- 30 yd. (28 m) worsted weight yarn
- Size H/8 (5.00 mm) crochet hook
- Scissors
- Yarn needle
- Knitter's pin or marker

Skills

- Make a chain
- Plain single crochet
- Sew a seam

Finished size of hat:

- 10" (25 cm) circumference and 4" (10 cm) high

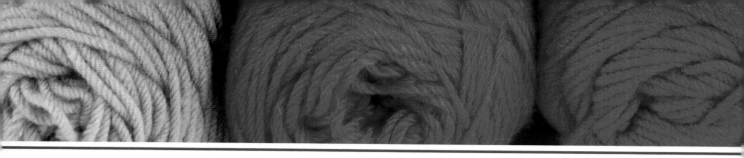

A Yarn Kid Hat and Scarf

The Hat

Make a chain that will go around your doll's head. Skip 2 stitches in the first row (it will stretch to fit).

Row 1: Skip the first 2 chains and single crochet in the third chain from the hook. Single crochet in each chain across. Turn.

Row 2: Chain 1, single crochet in every single crochet across. This is the right side. Place a marker on it. Turn.

Row 3: Chain 1, single crochet across. Turn.

Repeat as for Row 3 until your hat is tall enough to cover your doll's head. End off, leaving enough yarn to sew the side edges together.

Sew the side seam using an overcast stitch. (Your seam can be at the side or back of the hat.) Then choose any of the following steps:

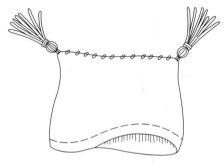

1. Overcast stitch the hat closed by sewing straight across the top.

2. Overcast stitch straight across the top, then sew the two points together.

3. Pull the top together at four equally spaced points. Tack them together with a couple of stitches.

Add chain ties, tassels or pompoms.

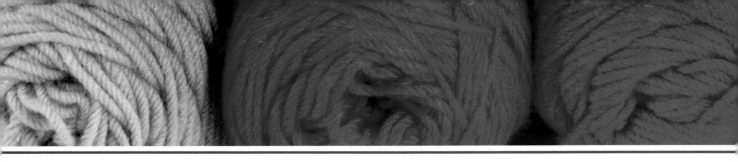

Making Pompoms

The easiest way to make pompoms is to simply wrap yarn around a piece of cardboard. The instructions below make a pompom about 2" (5.00 cm) across. A pompom this size works for most of the projects in this book.

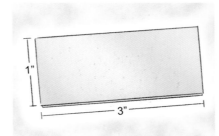

1. Cut a piece of cardboard 3" (7.50 cm) long and 1" (2.50 cm) wide.

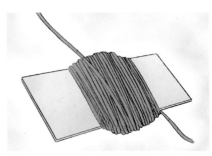

2. Using worsted weight yarn, make 60 wraps around the short side of the cardboard, keeping the wraps in the center third of the cardboard.

3. Tie a length of yarn around the wrapping at one edge of the cardboard. Allow enough length for tying your pompom to your project. (Pull the yarn through tight, wrapping with a crochet hook or a needle.)

4. Slip the wrapping off the cardboard. Pull the tie-off yarn around the wrapping that was at the edge of the cardboard again. Make a second knot so your pompom is secure.

5. Cut the loops on the opposite side of the tie.

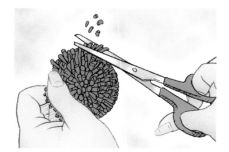

6. Trim the ends even.

Materials

- Yarn: Any, although you may want to start with a worsted weight
- Cardboard: Cereal box cardboard will work well if you don't wrap too tightly
- Scissors

Note: Use any yarn you desire for your pompoms. Make them soft and floppy with small amounts of yarn or very thick and puffy with more yarn. For variations, try multiple colors and types of yarn in a single pompom, or start with a smaller piece of cardboard to a make a doll-sized pompom. Trim to your desired length. The instructions state the number of wraps for an average size pompom in worsted weight yarn.

You can purchase a variety of pompom makers. One version consists of two plastic circles with holes in the center. It produces thick, even pompoms in a variety of sizes.

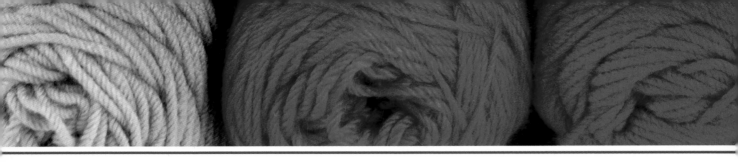

Making Tassels

Like pompoms, tassels can be made by wrapping yarn or thread around cardboard. The hat tassels for the yarn kid hat are 2½" (5.00 cm) long

1. Cut a piece of cardboard the length of your desired tassel and wide enough to hold in your hand and wrap the yarn.

2. Using worsted weight yarn, wrap 12 times around the long side.

3. Tie a length of yarn around the wrapped strands at one edge of the cardboard. Allow enough length for tying your tassel to your project.

4. Slip the wrapping off the cardboard.

Materials

- Yarn: Any, although you may want to start with worsted weight yarn
- Cardboard: Cereal box cardboard will work well if you don't wrap too tightly
- Scissors
- Yarn needle

Note: You can make your tassels any way you like. They can be thick or thin, one color or many colors. The instructions state the number of wraps for an average-sized tassel made with worsted weight yarn.

Tassel makers also are available from craft stores or online.

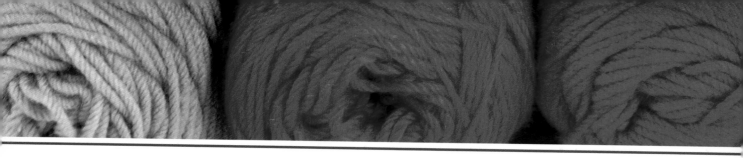

Making Tassels

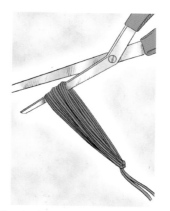

5. Cut the loops on the opposite side of the tie.

6. Make a "neck" by tightly wrapping a piece of yarn around the tassel, a short distance below the first tie. Tightly wrap in a section of your starting end.

7. When you are finished wrapping, thread the working end into a yarn needle and sew it securely into the wrapping.

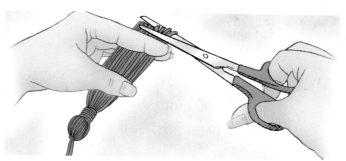

8. Trim the ends.

Chapter 3

Colors are wonderful playthings! Scientists and artists alike have been drawn to the questions of what is color, where does it come from and how can it be used. Most of us don't think to ask these heady questions, but we love to try different ways of bringing color together and trying new combinations of colors.

Color Ado

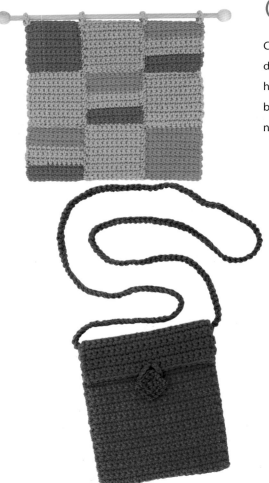

The projects in Chapter 3 are very simple shapes, squares and rectangles, but they each employ a different way to use color. The Twisted Potholder requires crocheting two strands of yarn at the same time. This method "blends" colors, almost like paints. The Possibilities Bag is worked in "color block" — each part is a different color. The Design Kit offers a way to play with solid colors and simple stripes. These projects provide a good excuse to look beyond local chain stores for yarn. Pay a visit to your nearest yarn store or order from yarn catalogs. Yarns from these sources often cost more, but you will find they can be good sources for a broader palette of colors. I occasionally use yarns from completely different sources together in the same project if I know their fiber content and size are the same. That way, I increase my color range even more.

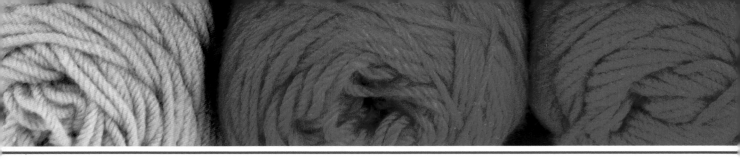

Fun and Useful Facts About Color

1. A good way to remember the rainbow colors in order is by using the name ROY G. BIV: red, orange, yellow, green, blue, indigo and violet. Sir Isaac Newton was the first person to label colors this way.

2. Newton also was the first person to create a color wheel. He did this by joining his labeled rainbow colors in a ring. The connecting color is violet.

3. Colors that are opposite each other in the color wheel will "complement" each other: orange complements blue; green complements red; violet complements yellow.

4. Analogous colors are right next to each other in the color wheel. For example: orange, orange-yellow and yellow. Analogous colors are especially easy to blend.

5. Cool colors like blue and green tend to look further away, while warm colors like red and orange jump out at you.

6. An item made in a warm color will appear even warmer if its texture is fuzzy or woolly. Likewise, a smooth texture will increase the cool effect of an item made in greens and blues.

7. The colors you surround yourself with reflect your personality.

The next three projects are all designed to provide easy, yet different, ways to play with color. Feel free to experiment and enjoy yourself!

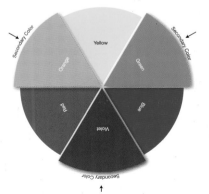

Primary colors.

Intermediate colors.

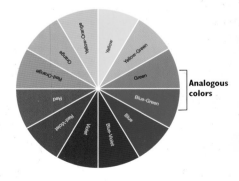

Analogous colors

Primary colors plus secondary tertiary colors.

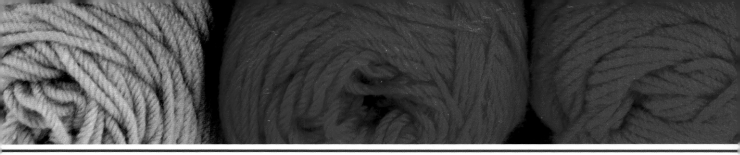

Slip Stitch
(Not the same as the Slip Knot)

Slip stitches are not as tall as single crochet stitches. They have a number of uses, one of which is connecting your work into a circle or cylinder.

1. Insert the hook into the stitch where your slip stitch will be placed.

2. Yarn over and pull through the stitch and the loop on the hook.

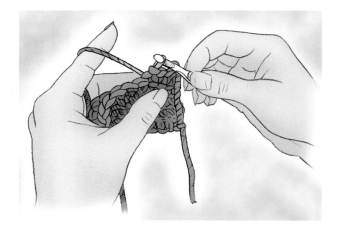

Changing Colors

1. Work the last stitch of the old color until the last step (two loops on the hook) drop the old color to the back and yarn over with the new color.

2. Draw the new color through the two loops.

3. You are ready to make the next stitch with the new color. Leave the ends 6" (15.0 cm) long for threading in later.

Change colors either in the middle or at the end of a row, or use this technique to add in new yarn.

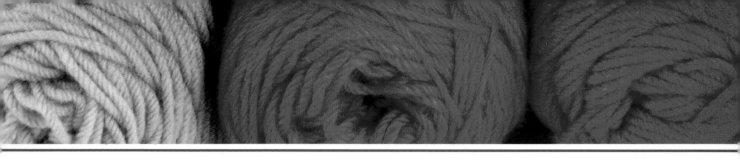

Twisted Potholder

Crochet two strands of yarn
together to make this thick,
useful square. Try all kinds
of color combinations and even
some textural ones. Give them
to friends, fill the kitchen drawer
or display your handiwork by
hanging them up for everyone to
admire.

Holding both strands of yarn together, make a slip knot and place it on your hook. Make a chain that is 5½" (13.75 cm) long, then add 2 more chains.

Row 1: Skip 2 chains, single crochet in the third chain from the hook and in each chain across. Turn.

Row 2: Chain 1, single crochet in each stitch across the row. Turn.

Repeat Row 2 until your potholder is 5½" (13.75 cm) tall.

Chain 12 for the loop. Slip stitch in the same stitch of the last single crochet to anchor the loop. Fasten off and weave in the ends.

Materials

- 35 yd. (21 m) each of two worsted weight yarns
- Size H/8 (5.00 mm) crochet hook
- Scissors
- Yarn needle

Skills

- Make a chain
- Plain single crochet with two strands

Note: Wind your yarn into balls and put each one in a separate container, such as a grocery bag or a bowl. Your project will proceed more smoothly.

Finished size:

- 5½" square (13.75 cm)

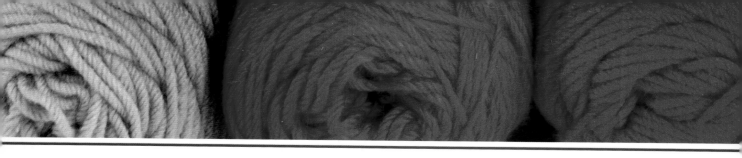

Possibilities Bag

What can you possibly carry in a small shoulder bag? An energy bar? A game? A small crochet project? This little bag has endless possibilities. It's worked in a color-block scheme (a different color for each part) and has a 4 by 4 piece to use as a button.

Materials

- 45 yd. (41 m) of two colors worsted weight yarn (front and back)
- 15 yd. (14 m) worsted weight yarn (flap)
  (All three colors should be the same brand.)
- Size G/6 (4.25 mm) crochet hook
- Knitter's pin or marker
- Yard stick or measuring tape
- Scissors
- Yarn Needle

Skills

- Make a chain
- Plain single crochet
- Change colors
- Sew a seam

Size

- Your finished bag will be approx. 6" (15.0 cm) wide x 7" (17.5 cm) long

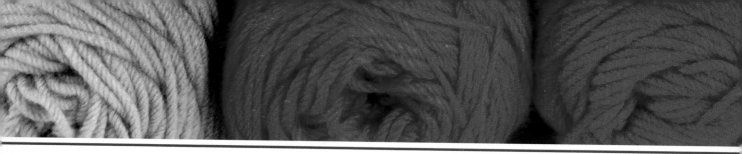

Possibilities Bag

Counting Rows

Plain Single Crochet

In plain single crochet, every other row looks different. One row looks like little v's and the next row looks like v's with short, horizontal strands across the tops. Learn to identify rows to be able to count them. There also are shallow furrows in the plain single crochet fabric with a row of stitches that look like v's and a row of stitches that look like v's with horizontal strands between them. It is easy to count rows by twos between these furrows. Don't forget to count any extra rows at the beginning or end of your work.

Leave a 14" (35 cm) tail for sewing one side seam. Chain 24 with the first color.

Row 1: Skip 2 chains, single crochet in the third chain from the hook and in each chain across (22 stitches). Turn.

Row 2: Chain 1, single crochet across. This is the right side of your bag. Mark it with a pin or marker. Turn.

Rows 3-30: Chain 1, single crochet across. Turn. Change to the second color at the end of Row 30.

Rows 31-60: Chain 1, single crochet across. Turn. Change to the third color at the end of Row 60. Leave a 14" (35 cm) tail of the second color for sewing the side seam.

Rows 61-70: Chain 1, single crochet across. Turn. Fasten off.

With the right side out, fold the bag so the first color is the front, the second color is the back and the third color is the flap. Overcast stitch the sides closed.

The handle: Cut a 15 yd. (13.65 m) strand of yarn and double it. Make a slip knot in the doubled strand and put it on your hook. Make a single crochet into the top edge of one side seam, chain until you have a handle 46" (115 cm) long and single crochet 1 in the opposite seam. Fasten off and thread the ends in.

The closure: If desired, sew a 4-stitch by 4-row button onto the front. Make a chain to go around it. Pull the 2 ends of the chain to the inside of the flap. Tie them in a knot and thread the ends in.

Fill with some take-along goodies!

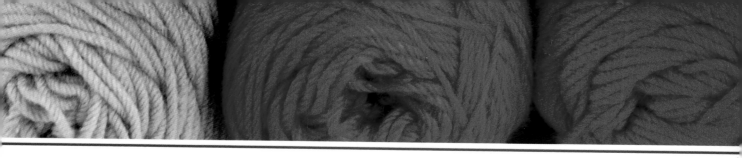

Design Kit

Wow! You've just learned how to crochet and you already want to be a designer! Designers spend a lot of time making small pieces called "swatches" to see what their ideas will look like in a certain yarn or color. Here are three specially designed swatches that allow you to experiment with both color and pattern. Make a collection of squares, lay them in front of you and move around for visual ideas, or sew them together to make potholders, hot pads or even a wall hanging.

Swatch 1

With one color, chain 14.

Row 1: Skip 2 chains, single crochet in the third chain from the hook and in each chain across (12 stitches). Turn.

Row 2: Chain 1, single crochet across. Turn.

Rows 3-12: Work as for Row 2. When you finish Row 12, measure the width and height of your square. If it is shorter than it is wide, add another row of single crochet. Fasten off. Thread in the ends.

Swatch 2

With one color, chain 14.

Row 1: Skip 2 chains, single crochet in the third chain from the hook and in each chain across (12 stitches). Turn.

Row 2: Chain 1, single crochet across. Turn.

Rows 3-6: Work as for Row 2, changing to the second color at the end of Row 6.

Rows 7-12: Continue to work as for Row 2 using the second color.

As with Swatch 1, add another row of single crochet, if necessary, to make the piece square. Fasten off. Thread in the ends.

Materials

- 100 g ball each of 3 different colors worsted weight yarn
- Size H/8 (5.00 mm) crochet hook
- Ruler
- Scissors
- Yarn needle

Skills

- Make a chain
- Plain single crochet
- Change colors
- Sew seams

Size

- 3½" square (8.75 cm)

Note: Achieve the best results by using the same yarn weight and same brand and hook size for each square. It is a good idea to keep all the materials for this project together.

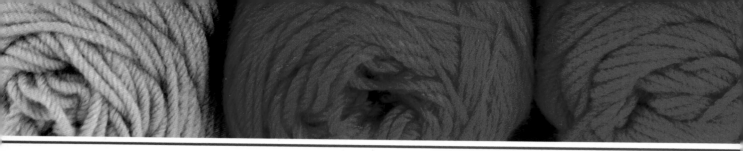

Design Kit

Swatch 3

With one color, chain 14.

Row 1: Skip 2 chains, single crochet in the third chain from the hook and in each chain across (12 stitches). Turn.

Row 2: Chain 1, single crochet across. Turn.

Rows 3-4: Work as for Row 2, changing to the second color at the end of Row 4.

Rows 5-8: Continue to work as for Row 2 using the second color. Change to the third color at the end of Row 8.

Rows 9-12: Continue to work as for Row 2 using the third color.

As with the other two swatches, add another row of single crochet, if necessary, to make the piece square. Fasten off. Thread in the ends. Lay the squares flat and sew together with an overcast stitch.

Overcast Stitch Two Pieces Laid Side by Side

1. Lay your pieces right-side up and next to each other.

2. Thread the yarn into your needle.

3. Pushing the needle from right to left, take a stitch in the corners of both pieces. A second stitch at the corners will help secure the sewing.

4. Continue to insert the needle in the top of the right hand piece and come up from underneath the left hand piece. Catch one strand of yarn on the edge of each side and match crocheted rows as you go. When you sew starting and ending rows, match stitch for stitch.

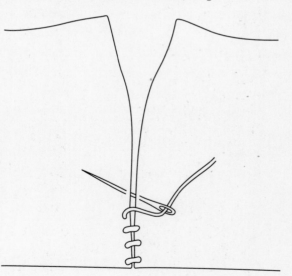

Ideas:

- Use heavy-weight yarn and a large hook to make a rug.
- With worsted weight yarn and a size J/10 (6.00 mm) hook, make a lap robe.
- A hook larger than size H/8 (5.00 mm) makes a more supple fabric.
- Baby sport yarn and a size H/8 (5.00 mm) hook will make a cute baby blanket.

Chapter 4

Need stretch? Back loop single crochet is a regular single crochet stitch worked into a different place. It makes a soft, stretchy ribbed fabric that can be used many ways. Front loop single crochet makes a slightly lacy fabric with rows of free loops traveling across it. One stitch — three different effects! Back loop single crochet makes a little front porch and

Back and Front Porch Loops

front loop single crochet makes the back porch. Try it and see! Chapter 4 also includes your first introduction to gauge and your first project using sport weight yarn. Gauge is the term for the method used to make crocheted items the correct size.

By now you have probably started to acquire a collection of crochet tools and need a place to organize your hooks. Hook Roll will help you do that. It is another reason for a gleeful excursion to find colors and textures — table napkins come in an amazing assortment. Make lots of hook rolls and share your love of crochet with friends!

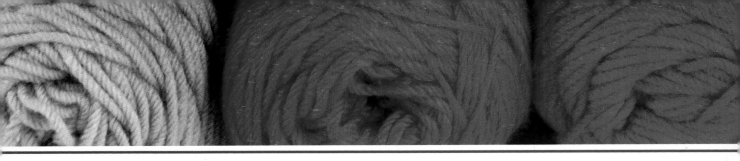

Make Back Loop and Front Loop Stitches

Back loop and front loop stitches are made the same way as a regular single crochet stitch, except the hook is not inserted under both loops. No matter which kind of single crochet you are making, you will first work a row of plain single crochet, turn your work and chain one.

Back Loop Single Crochet

1. Look at the tops of the stitches in your first row. Find the loops that look just like the front of a starting chain.

2. Skip the turning chain as you would for any other row. Insert the hook into the center of the chain of the next stitch and under the half that is furthest from you. Yarn over.

3. Pull up a loop.

4. Yarn over again.

5. Pull through both loops.

One back loop single crochet made! Working in the back loop of every stitch on every row produces crocheted ribbing.

Front Loop Single Crochet

1. Look at the tops of the stitches in your first row. Find the loops that look just like the front of a starting chain.

2. Skip the chain next to the hook. Insert the hook into the center of the top of the first stitch from underneath the loop closest to you. Yarn over.

3. Pull up a loop.

4. Yarn over again and pull through both loops.

One front loop single crochet made! Working in the front loop of every stitch in every row creates a lacy form of single crochet with rows of free loops on both sides.

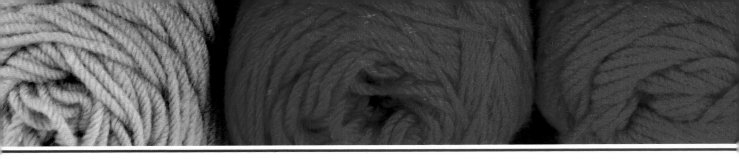

Snowflake Ski Band

What's warm and hugs your ears on a nippy day, yet easily fits in a pocket until it is needed? This stretchy ski band answers the question nicely. Working back loop single crochet for a short distance gives it extra stretch, and it's a quick-and-easy practice project.

Measure straight around your head with a tape measure. Subtract 1" (2.5 cm). This will be the length of your ski band. Make a note of it.

With a size F/5 (3.75 mm) hook, chain 14.

Row 1: Skip 2 chains, single crochet in the third chain from the hook and in each chain across (12 stitches). Turn.

Row 2: Chain 1, single crochet in the back loop of each stitch across the row. Row 2 is worked on the right side. Place a marker on it. Turn.

Row 3: Chain 1, back loop single crochet across. Turn.

Repeat Row 3 until your ribbing is 4" (10 cm) long. End on a right-side row. Turn. Change to an H/8 (5.00 mm) hook. Chain 1, plain single crochet across the row. Turn.

Continue to work back and forth in plain single crochet on 12 stitches until your ski band is the required measurement. End on a right-side row. Don't end off.

Finishing: Fold your ski band in half so that the right side is inside. Turn. Chain 1. Insert your hook into both loops of the first stitch in the ending row and a loop of the starting chain directly across from it. Yarn over, pull through and complete a slip stitch (see page 58). Repeat 11 more times. End off.

Materials

- 75 yd. (69 m) worsted weight yarn (Will fit an average head up to 22" (55 cm)
- 1 skein embroidery floss
- Size F/5 (3.75 mm) and H/8 (5.00 mm) crochet hooks
- Knitter's pin or marker
- Scissors
- Tapestry needle

Skills

- Make a chain
- Plain single crochet
- Back loop single crochet
- Slip stitch a seam

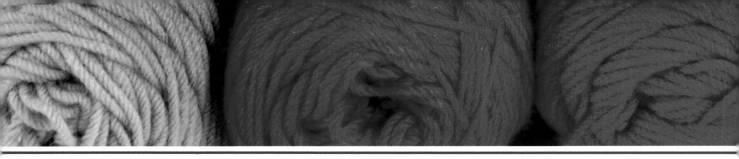

Snowflake embroidery:
(The large snowflake)

Decorate your ski band with light airy snowflakes using the fern stitch and either white or white with sparkles embroidery floss. Look at the last frame first and judge the placement of the stitches in the first five frames. See the photo of the ski band for ways to represent smaller snowflakes.

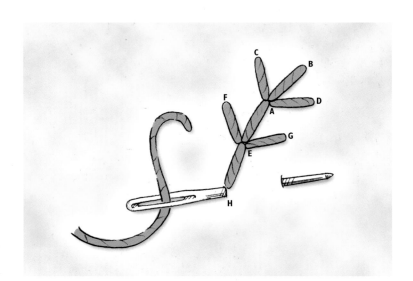

1. Come up at A, down at B.

2. Come up at C, down at A.

3. Come up at D, down at A.

4. Come up at E, down at A.

5. Come up at F, down at E.

6. Step 5 starts the second part of the fern stitch. Complete the third stitch of the second part of this fern stitch (come up at G, down at E). Add the extra stem (come up at H, down at E). This completes one of six arms for the snowflake, each consisting of two fern stitches (three straight stitches radiating from a central point) and an extra stem.

Back view of ribbing.

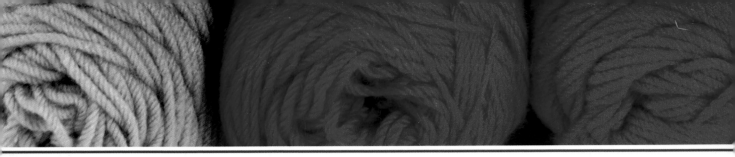

Cat Mat

Kitties of all ages and sizes love a soft nest. And all the better if it has its own toy permanently attached. This simple, square mat incorporates back loop ribbing as a border and an easy buttonhole space for the short, braided plaything. You can make Cat Mat in three sizes, from kitten to fat cat. As kitties also love clean places, it is a good idea to make it in a washable yarn.

Crochet a chain the required length of your desired cat mat plus 2 stitches. Your finished mat will probably be a little larger or smaller than your chain, but this project doesn't need to be exact.

Row 1: Skip 2 chains, single crochet in the third chain from the hook and in each chain across. Turn.

Row 2: Chain 1, back loop single crochet across. This is a right-side row. Place a marker on it. Turn.

Rows 3-6: Chain 1, back loop single crochet across. Turn.

Row 7: Chain 1, back loop single crochet 5, plain single crochet to 5 stitches from the end of the row, back loop single crochet 5. Turn.

Repeat Row 7 until the length measures 1" (2.5 cm) less than the width. Finish on a right-side row. Work the next 2 rows in back loop single crochet.

Make the buttonhole: Back loop single crochet 3, chain 2, skip 2 stitches in the row below, back loop single crochet in the next stitch and in each stitch to the end.

Next row: Back loop single crochet in each stitch including the 2 chains. Work 2 more rows of back loop single crochet. End off.

Add the tassel: Cut 12 pieces of yarn, 20" (50 cm) long. Pull the bundle of yarn through the buttonhole, dividing the length in equal units on both sides of the buttonhole. Divide all the lengths into 3 even bundles and braid them. Tie a tight overhand knot in the end and trim the remaining tassel. You also can wrap the end of the braid and securely thread in the ends, as with a regular tassel.

Overhand knot.

Materials for each size

- 12" (30 cm)
  - 202 yd. (184 m) washable worsted weight yarn
- 14" (35 cm)
  - 275 yd. (251 m) washable worsted weight yarn
- 16" (40 cm)
  - 360 yd. (328 m) washable worsted weight yarn
- 7 yd. (7 m) contrasting color, washable worsted weight yarn (for braid)
- Size H/8 (5.00 mm) crochet hook (I used a hook with a wide throat.)
- Knitter's pin or marker
- Measuring tape
- Scissors
- Tapestry needle

Skills

- Make a chain
- Plain single crochet
- Back loop single crochet

Sizes

- 12" (30 cm) square for kittens
- 14" (35 cm) square for adult cats
- 16" (40 cm) square for large adult cats

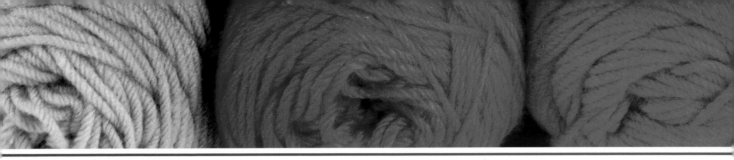

Cat Mat

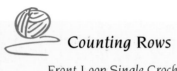

Counting Rows

Front Loop Single Crochet

Front loop single crochet creates rows of free loops running horizontally across your fabric. Count two rows between the rows of free loops, then count any extra rows at the beginning and end of your work. Two rows together will look as though there are rows of knots or little rosettes running horizontally. One row, by itself, will look like the small v's in plain single crochet.

Counting Rows

Back Loop Single Crochet

Back loop single crochet makes ridges with one row forming a more obvious peak than the next row. The rows are easy to count by twos, a complete ridge being made up of two rows. As with plain single crochet, don't forget to count any extra rows at the beginning and the end of your work.

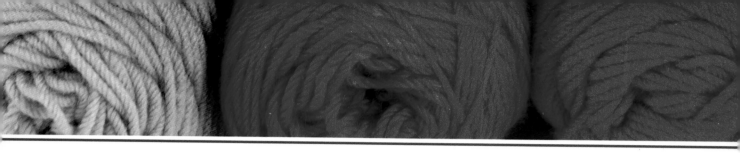

Dribble Bib

You know how messy babies can be! They need something to catch the drool and the food they can't keep in their mouths while they are still learning to eat. This soft bib can be wetted and used to wipe baby's mouth after the meal. It makes a great gift for a new mother. In this project, the back loop ribbing allows a square shape to conform to a baby's little, round neck.

The Body

With the color for the bottom of the bib, chain 39.

Row 1: Skip 2 chains, single crochet in the third chain from the hook and in each chain across (37 stitches). Turn.

Row 2: Chain 1, front loop single crochet across. Row 2 is worked on the right side. Place a knitter's pin or marker on it. Turn.

Row 3: Chain 1, front loop single crochet across. Turn.

Work as for Row 3 until your bib measures 4" (10 cm) long. End on a right-side row. Change to the second color to pull through the last two loops of the last stitch. Turn.

Materials

- 50 yd. (45.5 m) each of two coordinating cotton or cotton-blend yarns in sport weight or a light double-knitting weight
- Size F/5 (3.75 mm) hook (I used a hook with a narrow throat.)
- Measuring tape
- Knitter's pin or marker
- Scissors
- Tapestry needle

Skills

- Make a chain
- Back loop single crochet
- Front loop single crochet
- Change colors

Gauge

Bibs are good examples of items on which to practice a simple form of working to the gauge. Work a couple of inches in length, then measure across the entire piece to check if you have the correct measurement. The bib should measure 7" (17.50 cm) across.

Note: Instructions are given to work the bottom of the bib in front loop single crochet. Alternatively, you can work it in plain single crochet. Because single crochet is a little shorter than front loop single crochet, a measurement is given instead of a row count.

Finished size:

7" (17.50 cm) wide x 8" (20 cm) long

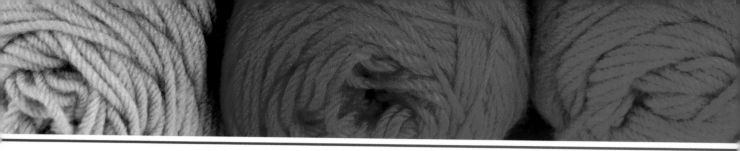

Dribble Bib

What is gauge?

Crocheters use a gauge for projects that are fitted (sized). Gauge is the number of stitches and the number of rows for an inch of crochet. Gauge may not be very important when you are making a simple item like a potholder or a beanbag, but when a perfect fit is required, your gauge will be extremely important. Small projects like baby items provide very good practice.

The Yoke

Rows 1-10: Chain 1, back loop single crochet across. Turn.

Row 11: Chain 1, back loop single crochet across. You will be ending on a wrong-side row. Turn. (Count 5½ back loop ridges on the front.)

Row 12: Chain 1, back loop single crochet in 11 stitches. Place a marker on stitch 12. Turn.

Left Shoulder and Tie

Rows 1-13: Chain 1, back loop single crochet 11 stitches. Turn.

Row 14: Chain 1, back loop single crochet 11. End on a right-side row, but do not end off. (Count 7 complete ridges on the front.)

The tie: Make a 12" (30 cm) chain. Turn. Skip 1 stitch, slip stitch in each chain plus 1 slip stitch in the side of the ending row. End off.

Right Shoulder and Tie

Make a slip knot with your second color and place it on your hook. With right side facing, complete Row 12 of the yoke by making a back loop single crochet in stitch number 12 (the one with the marker). Continue working back loop single crochet stitches across the rest of the row. Turn.

Rows 1-13: Chain 1, back loop single crochet 11 stitches. Turn.

Row 14: Chain 1, back loop single crochet across. Row 14 is a right-side row. (Count 7 complete ridges on the front.) Turn.

Row 15: Slip stitch in both loops of each stitch across the row. Do not end off.

The tie: Make a 12" (30 cm) chain. Turn. Skip 1 stitch, slip stitch in each chain plus 1 slip stitch in the side of the ending row. End off. Thread in the ends.

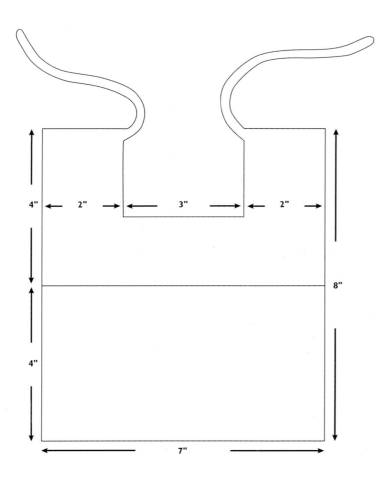

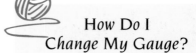

How Do I Change My Gauge?

Measure your bib. If your bib is too wide, choose any of the following options:

- Change to a smaller hook.
- Tighten the tension on your yarn.
- Change to a slightly thinner yarn.

If your bib is too narrow, follow these options:

- Change to a larger hook.
- Loosen the tension on your yarn.
- Change to a slightly thicker yarn.

It is easier to change your hook size. The same brand hook in the next size will work best. You may need to try more than one size larger or smaller.

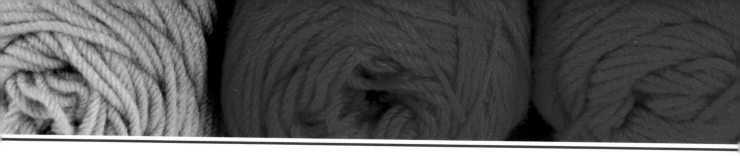

A Hook Roll

Get your hooks in a row! Use colorful, cloth table napkins to make organizing rolls for your crochet tools. For a special friend who crochets, a roll with several hooks and a measuring tape makes a great gift.

1. Fold one edge of the napkin up 5" (12.5 cm). Pin the sides and place several pins across the top of the pocket to keep it in place. Sew the sides.

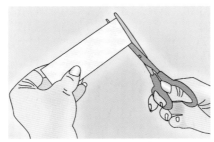

2. Cut a piece of lightweight cardboard 5" (12.5 cm) × 1½" (3.75 cm).

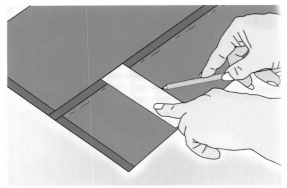

3. Use the pencil and cardboard to mark off 1½" (3.75 cm) wide pockets along the large pocket. Sew along the pencil lines, backstitching at the beginning and end of each stitching line.

Materials

- 1 cloth table napkin approx. 16" (40 cm) square
- Ruler
- Sewing pins
- ¾ yd. (.69 m) grosgrain ⅜" (1.0 cm) wide ribbon
- Graphite pencil
- Small piece of lightweight cardboard
- Thread to match napkin
- Iron
- Scissors
- Sewing machine (You can sew your hook roll by hand, but it will be more time consuming.)

Note: It is a good idea to wash, dry and iron your napkin before starting.

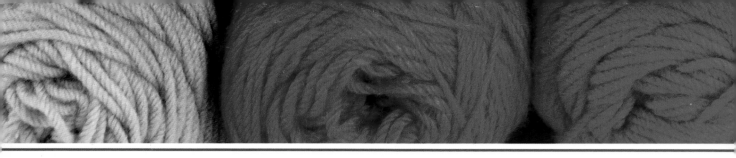

Hook Roll

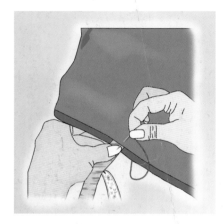

4. Fold the ribbon in half. Stitch the fold to one back edge of the pocket and 3" (7.5 cm) up from the pocket fold. Trim the ends of the ribbon at an angle. If you are using embroidered ribbon, turn it inside out and sew it to the pocket.

5. Wash out any dark pencil lines, if needed. Iron your hook roll smooth. Place your hooks in the pocket. Fold the top part down, roll and tie.

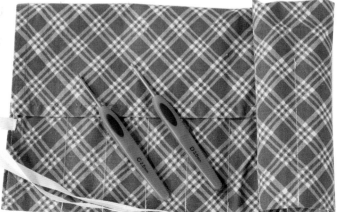

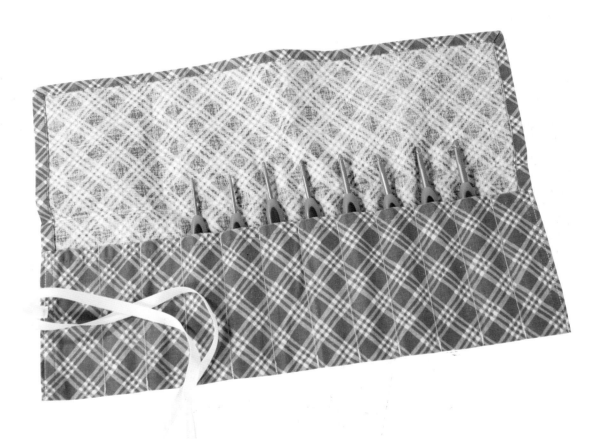

Chapter 5

Increasing and decreasing in single crochet is easy and opens up many design possibilities. This is the addition and subtraction of crochet. Take away several stitches and your work gets narrower; add stitches and it gets wider. Now you can shape hats to have a round end, sleeves to be narrow at the wrist and wider at the shoulder, not to mention crocheted creatures. I only made one critter for this book, but after you learn how to make Sheepish — what else? A pig, a dachshund, a lion?

More or Less Loopy

I included instructions for using the foundation stitch (single crochet with an extra loop and chain) to make a right angle increase for the CD Cube. This technique will create both your chain row and your first row of single crochet at the same time. It is much easier to use than the traditional technique for right angle increasing.

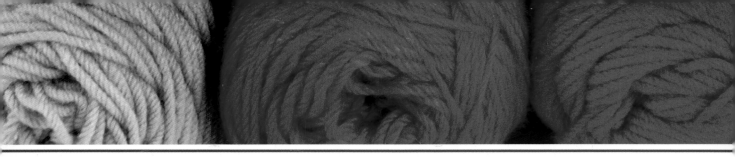

Increasing and Decreasing

Learn how to increase and decrease. The steps are easy to learn and definitely increase your ability to shape a variety of items in single crochet.

How to Increase

Work to the stitch where your increase will start. Make two single crochets in the same stitch of the row below. One increase made!

How to Decrease

Work to the stitch where the decrease starts.

1. Insert your hook, yarn over and pull through. Don't complete the stitch.

2. Insert the hook into the next stitch, yarn over and pull through. Now you have 3 loops on your hook.

3. Yarn over and pull through all 3 loops.

One decrease made!

Fun and Useful Fiber Facts

1. Yarns are spun from many different kinds of fibers. Some natural fibers, such as wool and silk, come from animals. Other fibers, such as cotton and flax, come from plants. There also are many man-made fibers, such as polyester, rayon and nylon.

2. Natural fiber usually feels better next to your skin when it is damp because it absorbs moisture better than synthetic fibers. For this reason, natural fibers have less static when the air is dry.

3. Wool will keep you warmer than any other fiber if you get wet while wearing it.

4. Angora comes from rabbits while mohair comes from Angora goats.

5. Silk has more tensile (pulling) strength than steel.

6. Alpacas, guanacos and vicuñas are all members of the llama family from South America. All three have very soft undercoats that make fluffy yarn.

7. Nylon is one of the most elastic synthetic fibers. Elastic means that if you stretch then release it, it will spring back to its original shape.

8. Wool is the most elastic natural fiber.

9. Cotton may have been used to make clothes as long as seven thousand years ago.

10. The use of linen can be traced as far back as the Stone Age.

11. Rayon was the first man-made fiber.

12. Items made from synthetic yarns are lightweight, strong and will dry quickly.

Silk, wool and angora yarns.

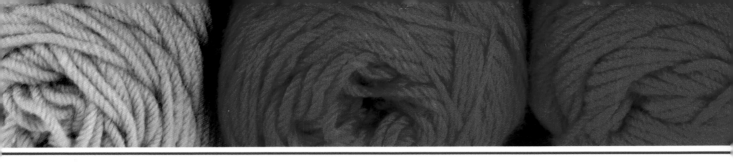

Bow Tie

It's a bow! It's a tie! It's an extra-easy-to-make bow tie that incorporates increasing and decreasing within a row. Make it yourself and you can choose colors to match anything you wear.

Put it in your hair, tie it around your waist or neck, or embellish anything you please. Try a shiny, metallic yarn for holidays or special occasions!

Leave an 8" (20 cm) tail, chain 12.

Row 1: Make a single crochet in the third chain from the hook and in each chain across (10 stitches). Turn.

Row 2: Chain 1, single crochet 10. Row 2 is worked on the right side. Put a marker on it. Turn.

Rows 3-10: Chain 1, single crochet 10. Turn.

Row 11: Chain 1, decrease by working 2 stitches together 5 times (5 stitches). Turn.

Rows 12-26: Chain 1, single crochet 5. Turn.

Row 27: Chain 1, increase by making 2 single crochets in each of the 5 stitches (10 stitches). Turn.

Rows 28-36: Work even on 10 stitches. End off leaving about 8" (20 cm) of yarn. Tie a knot in your tie on the wrong side. Shape it with your fingers. The knot should be centered on the right side and should have a smooth center. It should be crossed on the wrong side. Fold 2 rows to the back on each end, thread a tapestry needle with the tail of yarn and hem each side in place.

Push the piece of grosgrain ribbon under the crossed part of the knot on the back. Trim the ends of the ribbon diagonally to keep them from unraveling. Tie on your bow tie where desired and trim the ribbon as needed.

Materials

- 50 yd. (46 m) light worsted weight yarn (Cotton or cotton blends work well for this project.)
- Size G/6 (4.25 mm) crochet hook (I used a hook with a narrow throat.)
- Tapestry needle
- Scissors
- 1 yd. (.91 m) coordinating color grosgrain ribbon, ½" (1.3 cm) wide

Skills

- Make a chain
- Plain single crochet
- Increase
- Decrease

Size

- 5" (12.5 cm) long, after it is tied

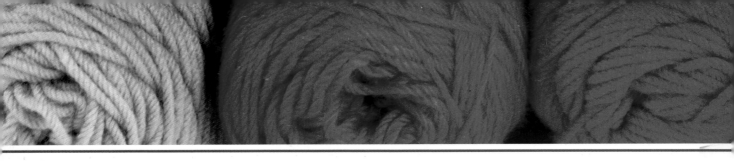

Cozy Scarf

Now that you know how to make simple increases and decreases within a row, you can shape this easy and practical scarf to be less bulky around the neck, yet provide great coverage on the chest. Cozy scarf is a variation of what is known as the "seaman's scarf."

Chain 25.

Row 1: Skip 2 chains, single crochet in the third chain from the hook and in each chain across (23 stitches). Turn.

Row 2: Chain 1, single crochet in each stitch across the row. Turn.

Repeat Row 2 until your scarf is 12" (30 cm) long.

Decrease Row: Chain 1, (single crochet 3, decrease 1) 4 times. Single crochet in the last 3 stitches (19 stitches). Place a marker on this row. Turn.

Work straight on 19 stitches until your scarf measures 22" (55 cm) from the marker.

Increase Row: Chain 1, (single crochet 3, increase 1) 4 times. Single crochet in the last 3 stitches (23 stitches). Place a marker on this row. Turn.

Work straight on 23 stitches until your scarf measures 12" (30 cm) from the last marker. End off.

Note: The parenthesis marks ( ) around instructions means you do everything inside them, the number of times it says, and in that order.

Materials

- 250 yd. (228 m) soft worsted weight yarn
- Size J/10 (6.00 mm) hook (I used a hook with a wide throat.)
- 2 knitter's pins or markers
- Scissors
- Yarn needle

Skills

- Make a chain
- Plain single crochet
- Increase
- Decrease

Size

- Your finished scarf should be 7" (1.75 cm) wide at the ends, 5¼" (13.13 cm) wide in the middle section and 46" (115 cm) long.

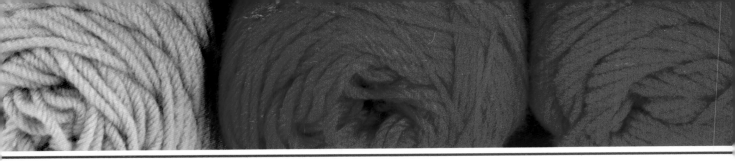

Cozy Scarf

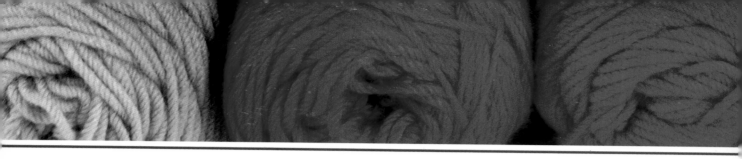

Baby Cap

"Baby Cap" is a small, simple project to make and provides a baby with soft warmth. It is worked flat and then sewn together for a short distance. This little hat pattern provides the crocheter with an opportunity to practice decreasing in the star-end pattern.

With the size G/6 (4.25 mm) hook, loosely chain 50.

Row 1: Skip 2 chains and single crochet in the third chain from the hook. Single crochet in each chain across (48 stitches). Turn.

Row 2: Chain 1, single crochet in the back loop of each stitch across the row. Row 2 is worked on the right side. Place a marker on it. Turn.

Row 3: Chain 1, back loop single crochet 48. Turn.

Rows 4-6: Work as for Row three. Change to the size H/8 (5.00 mm) hook.

Rows 7-18: Chain 1, plain single crochet 48. Turn.

Rows 19 and 20: Chain 1, back loop single crochet 48. Turn.

In the following rows, continue to raise a chain at the beginning of the row and turn at the end of the row.

Row 21: Plain single crochet across. You will be ending on a wrong-side row.

Row 22: Decrease 1, single crochet 5. Repeat across the row.

Row 23: Single crochet across.

Row 24: Decrease 1, single crochet 4. Repeat across the row.

Row 25: Single crochet across.

Row 26: Decrease 1, single crochet 3. Repeat across the row.

Row 27: Single crochet across.

Row 28: Decrease 1, single crochet 2. Repeat across the row.

Row 29: Single crochet across.

Row 30: Decrease 1, single crochet 1. Repeat across the row.

Row 31: Single crochet across.

Row 32: Decrease across.

Row 33: Single crochet across. End off, leaving about 10" (25 cm) of yarn. With a yarn needle, thread the yarn through the ending stitches. Pull them up and sew the side edges together as far as the ridge.

Materials

- 80 yd. (73 m) baby sport yarn
- Size G/6 (4.25 mm) and H/8 (5.00 mm) crochet hooks (I used hooks with wide throats.)
- Knitter's pin or marker
- Scissors
- Yarn needle

Skills

- Make a chain
- Plain single crochet
- Back loop single crochet
- Star-end decrease
- Sew a seam

Gauge

- Measured on the body of the hat; 8 stitches = 2" (5.0 cm)

  Note: See detailed gauge information for the Baby Cap on page 103.

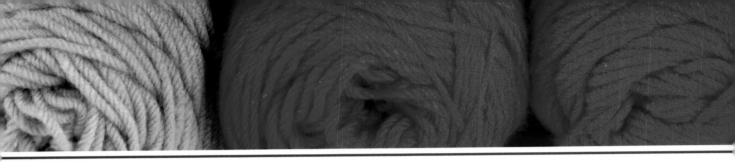

Baby Cap

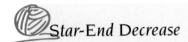 ## Star-End Decrease

The star-end decrease makes a smooth, round ending for hats, mittens and even bags. If you want to design a project with a round end in this easy and slightly spiraling pattern, you will first need to work out how many stitches are in your project.

Example: You have 29 stitches. Round to the nearest 10, which is 30. Divide 30 by 10 and you get 3 stitches between decreases. When you come to the place where you want to decrease, do the following:

Decrease 1, single crochet 3. Repeat across the row.

Single crochet the next row.

Decrease 1, single crochet 2. Repeat across the row.

Single crochet the next row.

Decrease 1, single crochet 1. Repeat across the row.

Single crochet the next row.

Decrease with no stitches in between. Repeat across the row.

Single crochet the next row.

A project with 82 stitches would start with 8 stitches between decreases and work a row of single crochet for the next row. You work one stitch less between decreases every other row with rows of plain single crochet in between.

Ties: Measure and cut 3 pieces of yarn, 1 yd. (.91 m) long, for each side. Pull the 3 strands through the 2 ridges on the inside front corners of the hat so the yarn is divided in half. Twist both strands clockwise, stopping every few twists to wrap the 2 strands around each other counter clockwise. Make the ties 12" (30 cm) long.

The Sweater Tee is worked to a gauge.

Gauge for Baby Cap

I love having small projects, such as the baby cap, with which I can learn about new yarns. If I use the same hook each time, but try different baby sport yarns, I can learn how the yarns will work to my gauge and what the fabric will feel like. If my cap turns out to be smaller or larger than my gauge, it will still fit a slightly smaller or larger baby. To perfectly fit a baby wearing a 0-3-month size, the cap will need to work exactly to the gauge.

Similar to checking gauge, as with the Dribble Bib, you can work about 2" (5.0 cm) in length and then measure the gauge. This time, instead of measuring all the way across, see how many stitches you have to the inch (2.5 cm). You should have 8 stitches across 2" (5.0 cm). Be exact. Even one half of a stitch will make a difference.

Measuring and Adjusting the Gauge

If there are fewer than 8 stitches inside of 2" (5.0 cm), start over with a smaller hook of the same brand.

If there are more than 8 stitches inside of 2" (5.0 cm), start over with a larger hook of the same brand.

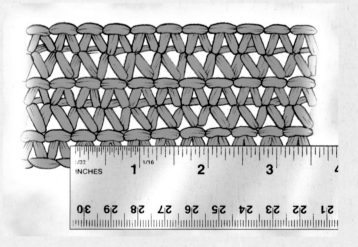

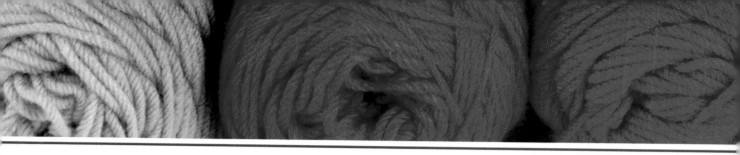

Sheepish

Whether you want a whole flock of woolly sheep or just one "bah," this cuddly toy is easy to make and doesn't need much care and feeding. The instructions to make Sheepish don't require a gauge. Make her in different sizes by simply changing the yarn and hook size. The largest sheep is made with super bulky yarn and is big enough to be a pillow. The smallest is made with fingering weight yarn and will be small enough to hang on a Christmas tree, or slip into a manger setting.

Materials for each size sheep

- Purchase the yarn weight and yardage for the size sheep desired. (I used Lion Brand "Wool Ease" products for all but the smallest sheep and crochet hooks with wide throats.

For each size sheep you will need the following:

- Size: 13" (32.5 cm) Sheepish
  - 84 yd. (77 m) white, cream or natural-colored super bulky yarn (body)
  - 55 yd. (51 m) black super bulky yarn (nose, ears, legs)
  - Size N/15 (10 mm) crochet hook
- Size: 10" (25.0 cm) Sheepish
  - 153 yd. (140 m) white, cream or natural-colored chunky yarn (body) 36 yd. (33 m) black chunky yarn (nose, ears, legs)
  - Size K/10½ (6.50 mm) crochet hook
- Size: 7" (17.5 cm) Sheepish
  - 197 yd. (180 m) white, cream or natural-colored worsted weight yarn (body)
  - 28 yd. (26 m) black worsted weight yarn (nose, ears, legs)
  - Size H/8 (5.00 mm) crochet hook

- Size: 5" (12.5 cm) Sheepish
  - 435 yd. (396 m) white, cream or natural-colored sport weight yarn (body)
  - 24 yd. (22 m) black sport weight yarn (nose, ears, legs)
  - Size F/5 (3.75 mm) crochet hook
- Size: 3" (7.5 cm) Mini Sheepish
  - 1 skein white, cream or natural-colored fingering weight yarn
  - Small amount black fingering weight yarn (nose, ears, legs)
  - Size B/1 (2.25 mm) or C/2 (2.75 mm) crochet hook
- Scissors
- Polyfil
- Size 13 yarn needle for super bulky and bulky yarns
- Size 16 yarn needle for worsted, sport and fingering weight yarns

Skills

- Make a chain
- Single crochet
- Decrease
- Change color
- Sew seams

Place a white cloth in your lap when working with very dark colors. The stitches will show up better.

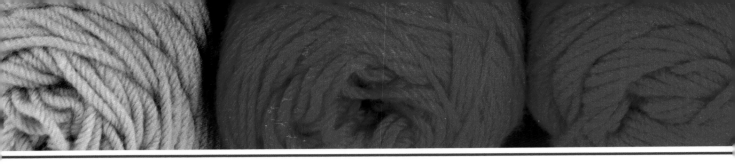

Sheepish

The Body

Chain 34.

Row 1: Skip 2 chains and single crochet in the third chain from the hook. Single crochet in each remaining chain (32 stitches). Turn.

Row 2: Chain 1, single crochet 32 stitches. This is the right side. Place a marker on it. Turn.

Row 3: Chain 1, single crochet across. Turn.

Rows 4-20: Work as for Row 3.

Rows 21-23: Chain 1, decrease 1, work to 2 stitches from the end of the row, decrease 1. Turn.

Row 24: Work as for Rows 21-23 to the last step of the last stitch. Change colors by pulling through the 3 loops with the black yarn. Cut the cream-colored yarn leaving a length for sewing. Turn.

Note: The general rule for sewing items together with an overcast stitch is as follows: The strand of yarn used to sew the items together should be three times the length of the item to be stitched.

The Nose

Rows 25-32: Working with the black yarn, continue as for Rows 21-23. End off, leaving a length for sewing.

The Legs

Chain 10.

Row 1: Skip 2 chains and single crochet in the third chain from the hook. Single crochet in each remaining chain (8 stitches). Turn.

Row 2: Chain 1, single crochet 8 stitches. Turn.

Rows 3-12: Work as for Row 2. End off, leaving a length of yarn for sewing. This piece will make two legs. Make another piece for the other two legs.

The Ears

Leave an 8" (20 cm) length for sewing and chain 7.

Row 1: Skip 2 chains and single crochet in the third chain from the hook. Single crochet in each remaining chain (5 stitches). Turn.

Row 2-5: Chain 1, single crochet 5 stitches. Turn.

Row 6: Chain 1, decrease 1, single crochet 1, decrease 1. Turn.

Row 7: Chain 1, double decrease. (Insert the hook into each of the 3 remaining stitches drawing up a loop each time, then yarn over and draw through all 4 loops.) End off. Make a second ear.

The Tail

Leave an 8" (20 cm) length for sewing. Chain 17.

Row 1: Skip 2 chains and single crochet in the third chain from the hook. Single crochet in each remaining chain. End off, leaving an 8" (20 cm) length to sew the tail.

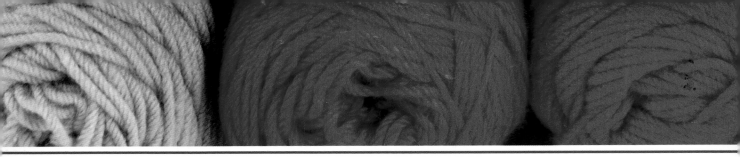

Sheepish

Sew "Sheepish" Together

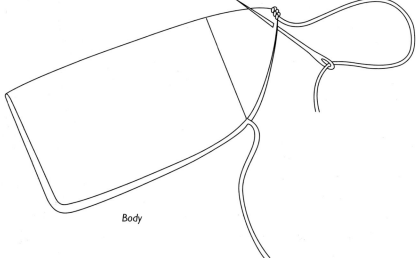

Body

Tail

1. Thread the yarn at the end of the nose into your tapestry needle and weave it through the ending stitches. Pull the yarn up to round the nose. Overcast stitch (see page 41 from the nose to the throat with the same yarn.

2. Thread the yarn in and cut it. Continue to overcast stitch the underside of the body with the cream-colored yarn. Sew half way up the back. Stuff the body. Make a few more stitches, then run the yarn in and out of the stitches around the remaining opening, going up one side and down the other. Pull the yarn up, rounding off the back.

3. Curve the tail into a flat U-shape and overcast stitch down the center. Thread in the end and cut it.

4. With the other strand, sew the tail to the back of the body. Thread in the end and cut it.

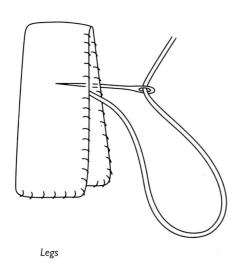

Legs

5. Thread one of the yarn ends from one leg piece into the tapestry needle. Fold the leg piece lengthwise. Overcast stitch down the long side and across the short side. One end should remain open. Push a little stuffing into the far end of the leg piece, leaving room for it to bend in half. Place another bit of stuffing in the opening. Sew the leg piece closed, starting with a new piece of yarn. Fold the leg piece in half to make two legs. Thread the yarn half way up the legs and sew them together, working toward the fold. This will enable your sheep to stand.

6. Sew the fold of the legs to the belly. Take a couple of small stitches at the beginning and end to secure the yarn. Thread in the ends. Trim. Sew the second leg.

7. Thread in the ending yarn at the tip of one ear. With the beginning yarn, sew the ear to the head. Try to curve the ear so it stands up. Refer to the photo for ear placement. Thread in the ends. Trim. Sew the second ear.

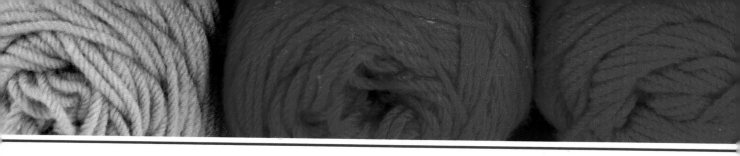

The Foundation Stitch

The foundation stitch enables you to make both the chain row and the first row of stitches at the same time. It is neater to work your chain row and first row, as shown at the beginning of the book, but the foundation stitch can come in very handy. I have found the foundation stitch is best used for making right angle increases. The instructions below explain how to work a row of foundation stitches that can be used for just about any single crochet project. There are specific instructions in the CD Box project for using this stitch to make a right angle increase.

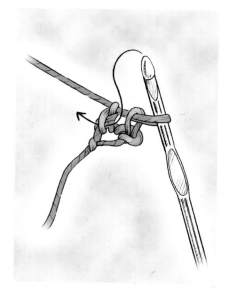

1. Chain 2.

2. Insert the hook into the second chain from the hook. Yarn over and pull up a loop.

3. Chain 1 in that loop. The loop that just fell away from the hook is your first base chain. Look at it closely so you can recognize it when you start the second single crochet.

4. Yarn over again and pull through the remaining 2 loops on the hook to finish the single crochet. Mark this first single crochet so you will recognize it after you complete the next row.

5. To make the second foundation stitch, insert your hook into your first base chain.

6. Draw up a loop, chain 1 in that loop, yarn over again, and pull through both loops on the hook to complete the second single crochet.

7. To make your third stitch, insert your hook in the second base chain, pull up a loop, chain 1 in that loop, yarn over and complete the single crochet. Continue as above.

CD Cube

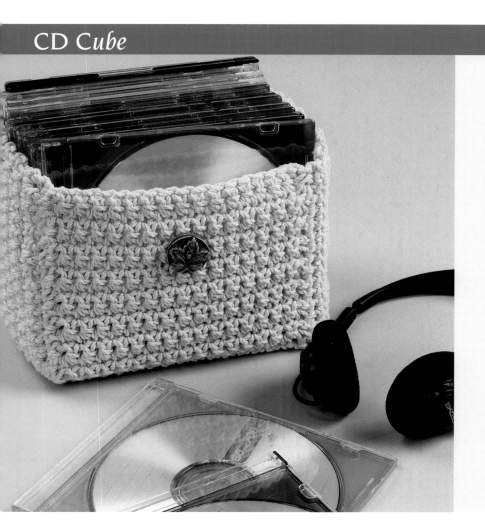

A crocheted box? Sure! This one has a pleasing basket-like texture and can be used to organize 10 CDs or several small books. The instructions explain how to crochet the cube flat, create right angle increases and sew the sides together. Once you know how, try designing different size boxes, a larger one to store colorful socks or a very small one in nylon cord for jewelry.

A hook with a wide throat is best because the cable cord is hard. A hook with a narrow throat may tighten the stitches too much, making it difficult to work.

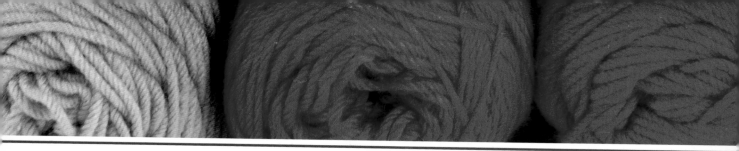

CD *Cube*

Materials

- 2 balls 60 yd. (55 m) cotton cable cord

  Note: This type of cord can usually be found at the hardware store. It comes in several sizes, but it's not clearly marked the way yarn is marked. The size required can be wrapped around a ruler exactly 11 times inside an inch.

- Size I/9 (5.50 mm) crochet hook
- Size 13 (7 cm) yarn needle
- Scissors

Gauge

- 8 stitches = 2½" (6.25 cm), 5 rows = 1½" (3.75 cm)

Skills

- Make a chain
- Single crochet
- Increase at right angles
- Sew seams

Pull the string from inside the ball. Leave an 18" (45 cm) tail. Chain 18.

Row 1: Skip 2 stitches and single crochet in the third chain from the hook. Single crochet in each chain across (16 stitches). Turn.

Row 2: Chain 1, single crochet across. This is a right-side row. Mark it. Turn.

Row 3: Chain 1, single crochet across. Turn.

Repeat Row 3 until you can count 16 rows on the right side of the work. Don't turn.

First Increase: Chain 18, turn, skip the 2 chains next to the hook, single crochet in the third chain and the next 15 chains (16 stitches). Work the next 15 stitches over the original square.

Second Increase: In stitch 16 of the original square, insert the hook, yarn over and pull up a loop. Make a chain in that loop (take note of what it looks like) yarn over and pull through both loops on the hook. You have just made a foundation stitch. *Insert the hook into one loop of the chain part from the last foundation stitch, pull up a loop, make a chain in that loop, yarn over and pull through both loops. You now have 2 foundation stitches. Repeat from the * until there are 17 foundation stitches (the last stitch of the square and 16 more). Turn.

Chain 1, work straight on 48 stitches until there are 16 rows in this section. End off.

Make a slip knot with your string and put it on the hook. With the wrong side facing, count 16 stitches in from the right. Single crochet in the next 16 stitches. Work straight on the middle 16 stitches until there are 16 more rows. End off.

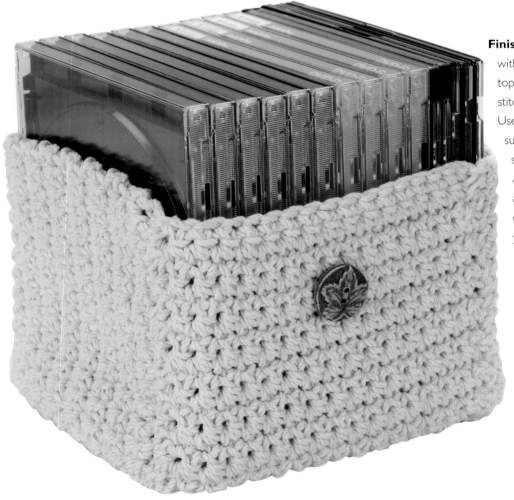

Finishing: Fold the piece into a cube with the right-side out. Starting at the top, with the edges even, overcast stitch down each of the four corners. Use the extra-large yarn needle suggested or use a sturdy, regular sewing needle and matching thread. A thimble may come in handy. Sew a great button or an interesting charm onto the front. Fill it up with your favorite possessions!

Chapter 6

"Go round and round the village." Spiral rows of stitches around in a tube shape to make a simple bath bag. Working single crochet in continuous rounds to make a tube is an important skill and creates yet another form of single-crochet fabric.

Loop the Loops

To work an object in a tube, with the look of plain single crochet, work back and forth in the round. Once you have accomplished this skill, you can embellish your work with textured patterns that aren't well suited to continuous rounds. You can make hats, mittens and bags that don't need seams. And, as with a scarf, you can make a fabric that matches plain single crochet worked flat.

Spiraling rows of stitches can be used to make flat circles as well as tubes. Start in the center, as with "A Shining Ornament" (page 124) and include the increase pattern each time you go around. What else could you make with a flat circle? Don't stop now. By the time you learn these skills you can do just about anything, and you'll be ready for the easy challenges in Chapter 7.

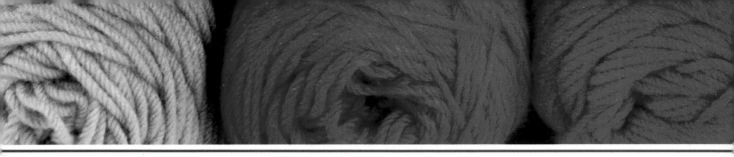

Join Yarn to Work in a Tube

The traditional way to join yarn, and start working a tube, is to join your starting chain with a slip stitch in the first chain. Making something with a long chain can be awkward to get started without twisting or tangling your chain. I always start a tube by making a first row of single crochet, then join the work with a slip stitch in the top of the first stitch of the row. The un-joined bottom of the row can be sewn together quickly and easily, before you thread in the end. There are two ways to join your work. In each case, the first stitch of the single crochet row is brought around to the left of the last stitch without twisting.

Join a Row of Single Crochet as to Work on the Outside

If your project calls for working continuous rounds on the outside, it makes sense to join the round as though to work on the outside. The tube will be behind your hands.

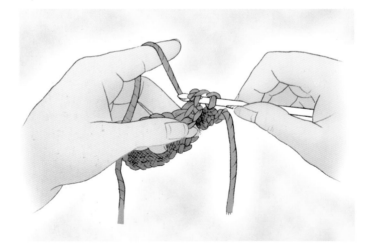

Join a Row of Single Crochet as to Work on the Inside

If your project calls for working back and forth in the round, and you want a smooth finish on the starting edge, join as to work on the inside. In this case, the tube is in front of your hands. After you slip stitch, chain 1 and turn. Work your second row as an outside row. Alternate inside and outside rows after that.

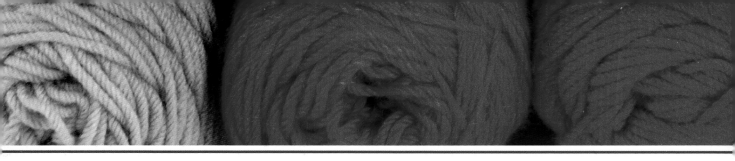

Soap Scrap Bag

Ever wish for a way to use up those last slivers of bar soap? Pop soap pieces into Soap Scrap Bag and use it as a scrubbie. Or, make one as a gift and enclose a scented bar of soap. Soap Scrap Bag is worked as a tube in continuous rounds.

Leave a 16" (40 cm) tail. With the main color, loosely chain 30.

Row 1: Skip 2 chains and single crochet in the third chain from the hook. Single crochet in each remaining chain (28 stitches).

Row 2: Without twisting, bring the front of the first stitch of the row around to the left of and next to the last stitch worked. You will be working on the outside of the tube. Slip stitch in the first stitch of the first row. Do not turn. Single crochet the next stitch. Continue to single crochet around using the starting tail as a row guide. The ends of the first row will be sewn closed later.

Rows 3-10: Single crochet around. Change to the second color at the end of Row 10. Work each color change above the starting tail. (Working in this method with plain single crochet gives the fabric a twist. It is better to use the starting tail as a guide rather than a marker.)

Rows 11-12: Single crochet around. Change to the third color at the end of Row 12.

Rows 13-14: Single crochet around. Change to the second color at the end of Row 14.

Rows 15-16: Single crochet around. Change to the main color at the end of Row 16.

Rows 17-26: Single crochet around.

Row 27: Chain 1 and skip 1 stitch in the row below, single crochet the next stitch. Repeat to the end of the row.

Finishing:

On the inside of the bag, knot the 2 strands together at each color change and thread in the ends.

Sew the bottom closed and tack the edges of the first row closed with an overcast stitch.

Make a 24" (60 cm) chain with the two accent colors. Thread it through the open stitches at the top of your bag.

Materials

- 50 yd. (46 m) sport weight yarn in cotton or a cotton blend (for a solid-colored bag)
- Small amounts of two coordinating colors of sport weight yarn (for accent stripes)
- Size H/8 (5.00 mm) hook (I used a hook with a wide throat.)
- Scissors
- Yarn needle
- Measuring tape

Skills

- Make a chain
- Plain single crochet
- Join a round to make a tube
- Work a tube in continuous rounds
- Change colors
- Sew a seam

Size

- Your finished bag will measure approx. 3¼" (8.13 cm) wide x 5½" (13.75 cm) long.

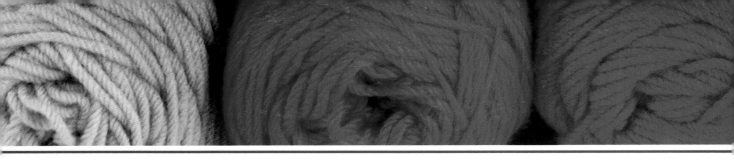

Tube Topper

Just like the hat for the Yarn Kids, here is a hat you can make for yourself or a friend. Choose from a variety of ways to finish the top. Instructions are given for working back and forth in the round so you won't have to sew a seam up the back when you finish crocheting.

There are two ways to make sure this project fits. The easiest way is to measure straight around the head (of the person for whom you are making the hat) and subtract 1" (2.5 cm). Make a chain the needed length (without stretching) and add 2 chains for the turning chain. Check for fit after you have worked several rows.

Another option is to make a 20-stitch by 20-row swatch. Measure your stitches to the inch, as shown on page 84. After you know how many stitches to make every inch with your hook and yarn, measure the head of the person for whom you are making the hat. Measure straight around at the forehead. Now subtract 1" (2.5 cm). Multiply the stitches per inch (measured on your swatch) times the inches you need. Add 2 stitches for the turning chain. The hat will stretch to fit.

Loosely chain the number of stitches you need and add 2 chains for a turning chain.

Row 1: Skip 2 chains, single crochet in the third chain from the hook and in each chain across. At this point, you can either work back and forth until your hat is tall enough and then sew the edges together, or follow the directions for Rows 2 and 3 to make a tube as you go.

Row 2: Without twisting your work, bring the first stitch of the row around and place it to the left of and next to the last stitch of the row, as though to work an inside row. Make a slip stitch in the first stitch, turn, chain 1. Skipping the chain next to the hook, make a single crochet in the next stitch. Place a marker in the top of this stitch and continue around in single crochet. As you complete the row, be careful not to single crochet in the stitch with the slip stitch from the previous row. Slip stitch in the first stitch of the round (the one marked). Row 2 is an outside row. Put a marker on it. Turn. (Tack the bottom of the first row together when your hat is completed.)

Materials

- 200 yd. (182 m) worsted weight yarn
- Size H/8 (5.00 mm) crochet hook
- 2 knitter's pins or markers
- Scissors
- Yarn needle
- Optional: pompom or tassel maker

Skills

- Make a chain
- Plain single crochet
- Join a round
- Work back and forth in the round to make a tube

Note: Try making a Yarn Kid hat, back and forth in the round, as a trial project.

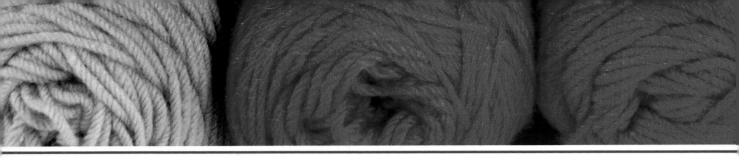

Tube Topper

Row 3: Chain 1, single crochet 1, replace the marker in the first stitch and finish the round ending with a slip stitch in the first stitch. Row 3 is worked on the inside of this hat.

Continue to work in this manner until your hat is tall enough to sew closed at the top. If you want a simple hat, without a cuff, sew it closed and finish it with tassels, pompoms or ties, as for the Yarn Kid Hats. You also can thread a piece of yarn, weave it through every third stitch, and draw it up.

If you would like a cuff, work about 6 more rows, then turn your hat inside out to finish. When you fold your cuff up the smoother side of the starting edge will show.

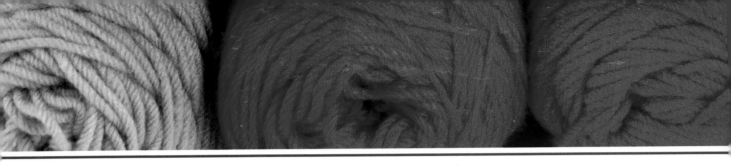

A Shining Ornament

Make a little holiday sparkle of your own and hang it where you wish! Try tying one or more to a gift package — two gifts in one. In the making, you will practice with a thin cotton strand and a small hook, learn about increases for a circle and work in continuous flat rounds.

Carefully count every round, or place a marker on the first stitch of each round. Chain 4 and connect with a slip stitch in the first chain.

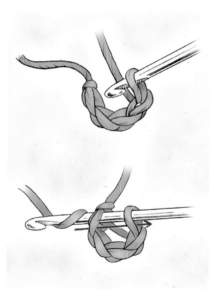

Round 1: Continue working to the left for each round. Make 5 single crochets, working each one into the center of the chain.

Round 2: Make 2 single crochets in each of the previous 5 stitches (10 single crochet).

Round 3: (Make 1 single crochet in the next stitch, 2 single crochets in the next stitch) 5 times (15 stitches).

Round 4: (Make 1 single crochet in each of the next two stitches, 2 single crochets in the next stitch) 5 times (20 stitches).

Round 5: (Make 1 single crochet in each of the next 3 stitches, 2 single crochets in the next stitch) 5 times (25 stitches).

Slip stitch in the next stitch. End off.

Materials

- 16.4 yd. (15 m) size 3 perle cotton
- 8.7 yd. (8 m) metallic gold or silver embroidery floss
- Size C/2 (2.75 mm) or D/3 (3.25 mm) crochet hook
- Scissors
- Size 18 yarn needle

Skills

- Make a chain
- Plain single crochet
- Join a chain
- Make stitches inside a joined chain
- Work in continuous flat rounds

Size

- Approx. 1¾" (4.375 cm) across the diameter

Note: You can work this project with heavier yarn if you don't feel you are ready to work with perle cotton.

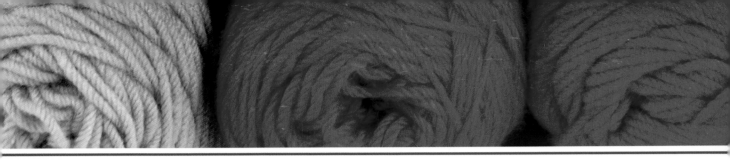

A Shining Ornament

Your ornament will have a slightly pentagonal or five-sided appearance. Keep the angled look by making the metallic row with 5 increases in the same pattern (4 single crochets and an increase every fifth stitch) or smooth it out by making your increases at random.

Leave a 6" (15 cm) tail. Make a slip knot in the metallic thread and place the loop on your hook. Make a single crochet in the slip stitch of the last row. Single crochet around, making 5 increases.

End off, leaving a 6" (15 cm) tail. Tie a knot in the starting and ending tails, then tie an overhand knot in the starting and ending tails, about 3" (7.5 cm) from your ornament. Trim the ends. Thread in any other ends. If necessary, narrow the hole that was left from working in the starting chain by threading the starting tail through those stitches with a needle and pulling them tight.

Chapter 7

Until now, it was as though you had a few puzzle pieces, maybe the border of a puzzle, put together. Then as you added more pieces (skills), you could start to see the picture develop. With Chapter 7, you see the whole picture. Now you can work back and forth in the round, increase, decrease a round end, make a pair of mittens,

Crazy About Crochet!

create crocheted ribbing, work the body of a hat on the ribbing and maybe even design your own hat. You also have developed the skills to measure and shape a simple garment.

The patterns included in this chapter are basic, but they each hold the possibility to do over and over, each time making something new. Use a new color or fiber, add stripes or work in blocks of color. As you continue to pursue and learn additional crochet stitches (half-double and double crochet) you can use these stitches to create texture.

Each of you will create something different — as unique and individual as you are. This is one of the joys of handwork. I hope you find that crochet becomes a favored form of handwork for you and you go absolutely crazy for crochet!

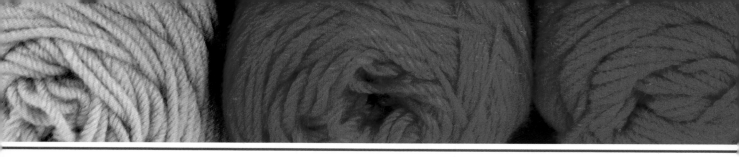

Sweater Tee

Basic and comfy are words that describe this wardrobe essential for a new baby. It is worked in plain single crochet with back loop single crochet borders. The sleeves are gently shaped. If you work it to the gauge, your sweater will fit most babies wearing a 0- to 3-month size.

 ## Gauge for the Final Projects

It is wise to make a gauge swatch of 20 stitches by 20 rows for each of the patterns in this chapter. It is necessary to make a gauge swatch for the vest since it is a full-sized garment. The number of stitches per inch and rows per inch are found after the materials list for each project. Remember to make your swatch from the same yarn and the same size and brand of hook that you will use for your project. Then measure and adjust as shown on page 103.

The Front

Chain 40.

Row 1: Skip 2 chains, single crochet in the third chain from the hook and in each chain across (38 stitches). Turn.

Row 2: Chain 1, back loop single crochet 38. Row 2 is worked on the right side. Place a marker on it. Turn.

Rows 3-6: Chain 1, back loop single crochet across. Turn.

Rows 7-34: Chain 1, plain single crochet across. Turn. Row 34 is worked on a right-side row.

Rows 35-39: Chain 1, single crochet 10, back loop single crochet 18, single crochet 10. Turn. Row 39 is worked on a wrong-side row.

Row 40: Chain 1, single crochet 10, back loop single crochet 3. Place a marker in the 14th stitch. Turn.

Materials

- 310 yd. (283 m) baby sport yarn
- Size H/8 (5.00 mm) crochet hook (I used a hook with a wide throat.)
- 2 coordinating ¾" (1.875 cm) buttons
- 5 knitter's pins or markers
- Yarn needle
- Scissors

Skills

- Make a chain
- Plain single crochet
- Back loop single crochet
- Increase
- Sew seams

Actual Size: 0-3 month

- Chest of sweater: 18" (45 cm)
- Back length: 9" (23 cm)
- Sleeve length: 6" (15 cm)

Gauge

- 8 stitches = 2" (5.0 cm), 16 rows = 3" (7.5 cm)

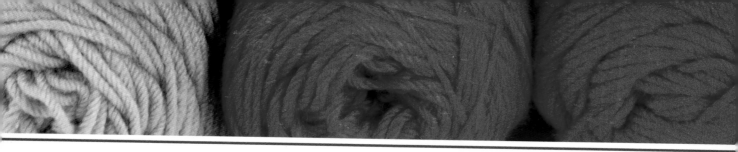

Sweater Tee

Left Shoulder

The left shoulder is the one that will be on the baby's left when wearing the sweater.

Row 1: Chain 1, back loop single crochet 3, single crochet 10. Turn.

Row 2: Chain 1, single crochet 10, back loop single crochet 3. Turn.

Rows 3-6: Repeat Rows 2 and 3 two more times. You will end on a right-side row.

Rows 7-12: Back loop single crochet across all 13 stitches. End off.

Right Shoulder

To complete Row 40 of the body, make a slip knot and place it on the hook. Working on the right side, back loop single crochet in stitch 14 (marked) and in the next 14 stitches (15 back loop single crochets) plain single crochet 10. Turn.

Row 1: Chain 1, single crochet 10, back loop single crochet 3. Turn.

Row 2: Chain 1, back loop single crochet 3, single crochet 10. Turn.

Rows 3-6: Repeat Rows 1 and 2 two more times. You will end on a right-side row.

Rows 7-12: Back loop single crochet across all 13 stitches. End off. Leave about 10" (25 cm) of yarn for sewing.

The Back

Chain 40.

Rows 1-6: Work as for the first 6 rows of the front.

Rows 7-46: Chain 1, single crochet across. Turn. Row 46 is a right-side row.

Rows 47-52: Chain 1, back loop single crochet across. Turn. You will end on a right-side row.

Gauge for Sweater Tee

As with the baby cap, this little sweater can be slightly smaller than the gauge and it will still fit a smaller baby, a preemie or a teddy bear. If it is larger than the gauge, it will still fit a larger baby. If you want it to exactly fit the average-size 0-to 3-month-old baby, your yarn and hook must work to the gauge stated for the pattern.

If you have already worked the baby cap with the same yarn and the same size and brand hook that you will use for the sweater, and you measured 8 stitches across 2" (5.0 cm), you can safely go ahead and start the sweater. If not, make a 20-stitch by 20-row gauge swatch and measure your gauge in the center of the swatch.

Check the gauge information on page 103.

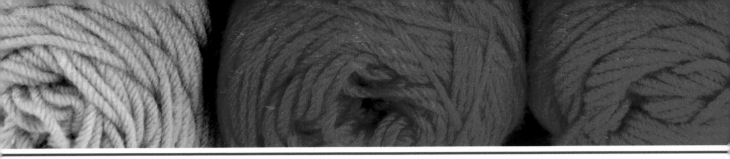

Sweater Tee

The Sleeves

Chain 32.

Row: 1: Skip 2 chains, single crochet in the third chain from the hook and in each chain across (30 stitches). Turn.

Row 2: Chain 1, single crochet in the back loop of each stitch across the row. Row 2 is worked on the right side. Place a marker on it. Turn.

Rows 3-6: Chain 1, back loop single crochet across. Turn.

Rows 7-13: Chain 1, plain single crochet across. Turn.

Row 14: Chain 1, single crochet 1, increase 1, work to 2 stitches from the end of the row, increase 1, single crochet 1. Turn.

Rows 15-21: Chain 1, single crochet across. Turn.

Row 22: Work as for Row 14.

Rows 23-29: Chain 1, single crochet across. Turn.

Row 30: Work as for Row 14.

Rows 31-32: Chain 1, single crochet across. Turn.

End off, leaving a length of yarn to sew the sleeve to the sweater body.

Make another sleeve.

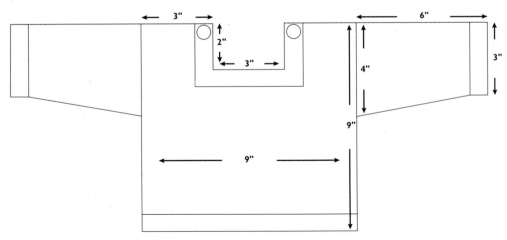

Finishing

Lay the top of the back and the top of the front together, edge to edge and right-side up. Work from the outside of each shoulder toward the inside. Sew about 6 stitches, using a ladder stitch, around the posts of the stitches.

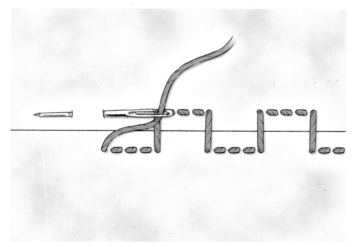

Ladder stitch.

For each sleeve: Lay all the pieces right-side up with the center of the sleeve matched to the shoulder seam. Count rows on the body of the sweater and match the corners of the sleeves to the same number of rows corresponding to each corner. Tie the sleeves in place with small pieces of contrasting yarn. Ladder stitch the sleeve to the sweater, working around the posts of sleeve stitches and picking up one or two strands from each row of the body.

Sew the underarm seams and side seams, matching rows and using an overcast stitch. Cut a piece of cardboard to fit inside the sweater. Place inside the sweater to make the seams lie flat while sewing.

Sew a button in the corner of each front shoulder. Attach a chain loop at the back of each shoulder.

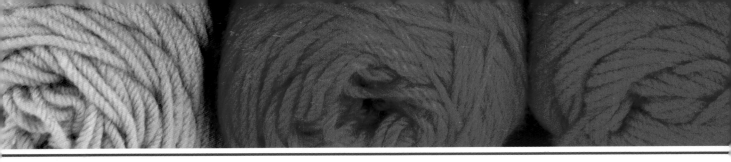

Knotty Hat

Make a hat with ribbing that
mimics knitted ribbing, shape the
crown with star-end decreasing and
then decorate it with "rug knots."
Your knots can be different shades
or textures of one color, many
colors, or any combination given
above. Make your hat very fuzzy or
only a little fuzzy. Have fun!

With the F/5 (3.75 mm) hook, chain 8.

Row 1: Skip 2 chains and single crochet in the third chain from the hook. Single crochet in each chain across (6 single crochets). Turn.

Row 2: Chain 1, back loop single crochet across. This is the outside of the ribbing. Place a marker on it. Turn.

Row 3: Chain 1, back loop single crochet across. Turn.

Repeat Row 3 until you have 103 rows (51½ ridges). You will end on a wrong-side row. Turn and chain 1.

Join the Ribbing

Fold the ribbing so the outside is inside and the chain row and ending row are aligned. Make a single crochet, inserting the hook into a chain of the starting row and a back loop of the ending row. Repeat 5 more times. Don't fasten off. Turn the ribbing right-side out.

Materials

- 150 yd. (136.5 m) worsted weight yarn
- Size F/5 (3.75 mm)
- Size H/8 (5.00 mm) (I used hooks with wide throats)
- Scissors
- Yarn needle
- Knitter's pin or marker
- Assortment of scrap yarns

Ribbing Gauge

- 1½" (3.75 cm) wide, 5 rows = 1" (2.5 cm)

Body Gauge

- 4 stitches = 1" (2.5 cm), 5 rows = 1" (2.5 cm)

Size

- This hat will fit a head up to 21" (52.5 cm) in diameter.

Skills

- Plain single crochet
- Back loop single crochet ribbing
- Join ribbing with single crochet
- Work into the edges of ribbing
- Work back and forth in the round
- Star-end decrease

Note: There is a detailed description for working back and forth in the round in Rows 2 and 3 of the Tube Topper. Instructions are on pages 121 and 122.

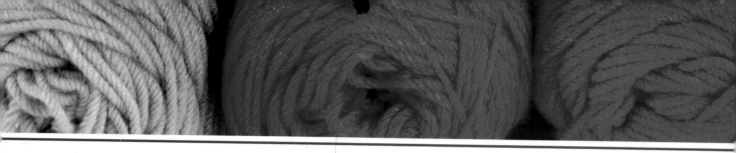

Knotty Hat

Work the Body of the Hat

Switch to the H/8 (5.00 mm) hook.

Row 1: You will be working in the ends of the rib rows and around the outside. Chain 1 and single crochet in the end of Row 1 of the ribbing. Place a marker on that stitch. Single crochet in the ends of Rows 2 and 3. Skip the end of one row. Continue to single crochet in the ends of 3 rows, skip 1 end row all the way around (78 stitches). Slip stitch into the first stitch of the round. Turn.

Row 2: Chain 1. From now on you will be working the body of your hat in both loops. Single crochet around.

Slip stitch in the first stitch of each round, turn, chain 1, single crochet and replace the marker in this first stitch of each round. Alternately work an outside row and an inside row until there are 16 rows. You will end on an inside row. Turn and chain 1.

Shape the Crown

Decrease 1 by working 2 stitches together, single crochet 8. Repeat to the end of the row. Single crochet any leftover stitches.

Single crochet 1 row.

Decrease 1, single crochet 7. Repeat to the end of the row. Single crochet any leftover stitches.

Single crochet 1 row.

Continue to decrease in the above pattern with rows of 6, 5, 4, 3, 2, 1 stitches between decreases and a row of single crochet after each one. After the row with 1 stitch between decreases, single crochet 2 rows without decreasing. With a yarn needle, draw the end of the yarn through the outside loop of every other stitch and pull up tightly. Thread the end to the inside and secure it.

Make a Rug Knot

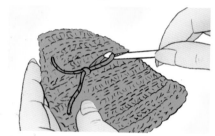

1. Insert the hook from the front of the hat around the post of a stitch and pull up the center of a small piece of yarn.

2. With the hook still in the loop you just pulled up, yarn over with the two ends and pull them through the loop. Tighten.

Randomly place as many knots as you like.

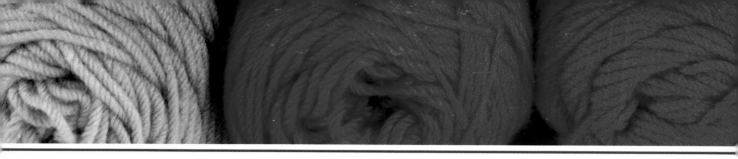

Striped Variation of Knotty Hat

You can work the body of this hat back and forth without joining the rows (you would have to cut and weave in ends, if you make single rows of color, and then sew up a seam) or you can work back and forth in the round. When working in the round, you make a variety of stripe patterns without cutting the yarn each time you change your color. Using the basic hat instructions, there are 16 rows in the body of the hat within which you can play with stripes. Start by making a few wrappings to preview your stripe layout, or just start in. You may want to work with only two colors at first. When you have finished your hat, work the first two rounds of the ornament project (page 125) in a matching yarn and make a button for the top of your hat.

Notes for Working Stripes Back and Forth in the Round

- Your yarn will be easier to work with when wound into balls.
- Yarns will twist around each other as you change colors. It will help to put each ball in a separate box or bag on the floor. That way, you can move the containers around to untangle the yarn. Untwist them every row or two.
- When you join a color from a new ball of yarn, drop the tail to the inside, but leave the yarn supply outside of your work.
- When you are ending a row and wish to change the color for the next row, complete the last stitch of the row with the color for that row, then drop the strand loosely to the inside. Insert the hook into the first stitch of the row, draw up the new color from the inside and slip stitch. Continue as for any other row. Turn and chain 1.

- At the end of inside rows, draw the yarn up from the inside and to a position behind the hook to yarn over for the slip stitch. It will feel a little awkward at first.
- There will be a "color seam" from your color changes.

Wrapping

Wrapping is a fast and easy way to preview which colors will look good together and in what proportions. It also is an excellent way to experiment with stripes. Try any combination of thin and thick stripes. Make wrappings just for the fun of it, or make them to help plan a crochet project.

Cut a piece of cardboard about 2" (2.5 cm) x 6" (15 cm). Wrap the colored yarn strands close to each other, but not overlapping. Work over loose ends. When you need to stop, cut a small slit in the cardboard and slip in the tail of the yarn.

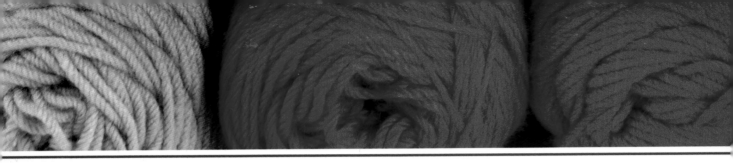

Mitten Times Two

With one pocket for the opposable thumb and one pocket for the other four fingers, mittens are warm winter-wear for hands. In some areas of Northern Europe mittens were considered important gifts and a valuable part of a woman's dowry. In making these mittens you will incorporate working back and forth in the round, increasing and star-end decreasing. The simple cuffs can be left plain or decorated with pompoms or interesting buttons.

Chain 30.

Row 1: Skip the first 2 chains and single crochet in the third chain from the hook. Single crochet in each chain across (28 stitches). Turn.

Row 2: Chain 1, single crochet in the next 28 stitches. Row 2 is worked on the right side of the cuff. Put a marker on it. Turn.

Row 3: Chain 1, single crochet in each stitch across. Turn.

Rows 4-8: Work same as Row 3. For contrasting cuffs, change the color at the end of Row 8 and turn.

Row 9: Chain 1, single crochet in next stitch. Place a marker in the top of this stitch. Single crochet in each of the remaining 27 stitches. Do not chain and turn. Bring the stitch with the marker

around to the left of the last stitch, as to make a tube with the right side of the cuff on the inside of the tube. The right side will be outside again when the mitten is complete and the cuff is turned up. Slip stitch in the stitch with the marker. Turn.

Row 10: Chain 1, skip the chain next to the hook, single crochet in the next stitch. Replace the marker in the top of the new stitch. Single crochet around, being careful not to work in the stitch with the slip stitch from the beginning of the row. Slip stitch in the stitch with the marker. Turn.

Rows 11-12: Work same as Row 10. You will be joining rows throughout the rest of the piece.

Materials
- Approx. 168 yd. (153 m) worsted weight yarn
- Size H/8 (5.00 mm) hook (I used a hook with a narrow throat.)
- 4 markers or knitter's pins
- Scissors
- Yarn needle

Skills
- Make a chain
- Plain single crochet
- Join a round
- Work back and forth in the round
- Increase
- Star-end decrease

Gauge
- 4 stitches = 1" (2.5 cm), 5 rows = 1" (2.5 cm)

Size
- When worked to the gauge, these mittens will fit an older child or a small adult.

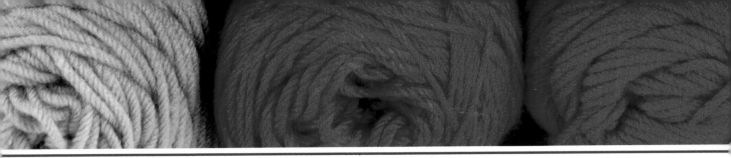

Mittens Times Two

Shape the Thumb Gusset

Note: For this pattern, increase rows are worked on the outside of the mitten and these are uneven numbered rows. The body of the mitten will be worked with the right side facing out.

Row 13: Single crochet in the next 13 stitches, increase by working 2 stitches in the next stitch. Place a marker in the first stitch of the 2 stitches; increase in the next stitch. Single crochet in the next 13 stitches (30 stitches).

Row 14: Single crochet around. Replace the thumb gusset marker in the new stitch on each row.

Row 15: Single crochet in 13 stitches. Increase in the next stitch, replacing the marker in the first of the 2 stitches. Work 1 single crochet in each of the next 2 stitches, increase in the next stitch. Single crochet in the next 13 stitches (32 stitches).

Row 16: Single crochet around.

Row 17: Single crochet in the next 13 stitches, increase in the next stitch, work 1 single crochet in each of the next 4 stitches, increase in the next stitch, single crochet in the next 13 stitches (34 stitches).

Row 18: Single crochet around.

Row 19: Single crochet in the next 13 stitches, increase in the next stitch, work 1 single crochet in each of the next 6 stitches, increase in the next stitch, single crochet in the next 13 stitches (36 stitches).

Row 20: Single crochet around.

Row 21: Single crochet in the next 13 stitches, increase in the next stitch, work 1 single crochet in each of the next 8 stitches, increase in the next stitch, single crochet in the next 13 stitches (38 stitches).

Row 22: Single crochet around.

Row 23: Single crochet in the next 13 stitches, increase in the next stitch, work 1 single crochet in each of the next 10 stitches, increase in the next stitch, single crochet in the next 13 stitches (40 stitches).

Row 24: Single crochet around.

Row 25: Single crochet around without any increases.

Row 26: Single crochet around.

Work the Palm

Row 27: Single crochet in 14 stitches and remove the marker; skip 12 stitches, single crochet in the next 14 stitches (28 stitches). The skipped stitches are the base for the thumb. They will be used after you complete the palm.

Work back and forth on 28 stitches until the palm reaches the tip of the pinky [about 3" (7.5 cm) or 14 rows]. End on an inside row.

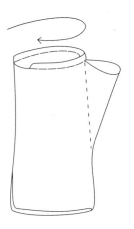

Star-End Decrease

Row 1: *Decrease by crocheting 2 stitches together. Single crochet in the next 3 stitches. Repeat from * across the row. Single crochet in the last stitch (22 stitches).

Row 2: Single crochet 1 row even.

Row 3: (Decrease, single crochet 2.) Repeat to the end of the row (16 stitches).

Row 4: Single crochet 1 row even.

Row 5: (Decrease, single crochet 1.) Repeat to the end of the row (11 stitches).

Row 6: Single crochet 1 row even.

Row 7: Repeat decrease across the row, ending single crochet in last stitch (6 stitches).

Cut the yarn, leaving an 8" (20 cm) tail end. Thread yarn into the yarn needle. Using needle, thread yarn through each remaining stitch. Pull yarn to close top of mitten. Thread yarn to the inside of mitten. Weave in yarn end and fasten.

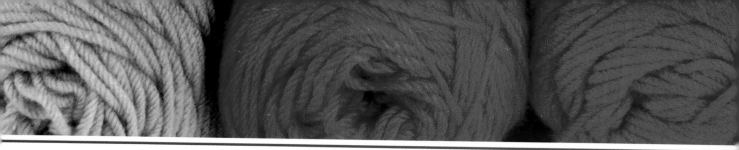

Mitten Times Two

Finish the Thumb

Leave an 8" (20 cm) tail and place a slip knot on the hook. Drop the tail into the thumb space.

Row 1: With the thumb gusset pointing up and to the left, single crochet in the stitch closest to the palm and put a marker in it. Single crochet in the remaining 11 stitches around (12 stitches). This is an outside row. Join the round in the top of the first stitch with a slip stitch. Turn.

Row 2: Chain 1, work the first single crochet and place a marker in this stitch. Single crochet in each of the next 11 stitches. Join the round to the top of the first stitch. Turn.

Rows 3-8: Work as for Row 2, continuing to join the rounds. You will end on an inside row.

Row 9: Decrease by working 2 stitches together all the way around.

Cut the yarn. With a yarn needle, thread it through each remaining stitch. Pull up, thread to the inside and fasten. Sew the small opening closed (between the thumb and palm) with the starting tail for the thumb. End off. Make another mitten!

Note: If you find it too difficult to work the thumb in joined rows, work it back and forth without joining, then sew it down the side, after you gather the top.

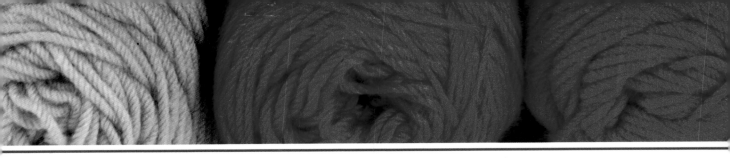

Vest

Here is the first full-sized garment! Simple shaping at the shoulders gives this vest a nice fit and drape. Bulky weight yarn yields a chunky, chill-chasing look while making the row count go quickly. Finish your vest with ties twisted from the same yarn, add buttons and loops, or sew on special Scandinavian style hooks.

Pattern is written for smallest size with changes for larger sizes in parenthesis.

Left Side Front

(The side that will be on the wearer's left)
Chain 20 (22, 23)

Row 1: Skip 1 chain, work 2 single crochet in the second chain from the hook. Place a marker in the top of the first stitch so that you will recognize it when you finish the second row. Single crochet in each chain across 20 (22, 23) stitches. Turn.

Row 2: Chain 1, single crochet in each stitch across. Row 2 is worked on the right side. Place a marker on it. Turn.

Row 3: Chain 1, work 2 single crochet in the first stitch, single crochet in each stitch across 21 (23, 24) stitches. Turn.

Row 4: Chain 1, single crochet in each stitch across. Turn.

Row 5: Chain 1, work 2 single crochet in the first stitch, single crochet in each stitch across 22 (24, 25) stitches.

Work even on 22 (24, 25) stitches until there are 30 (30, 32) rows total. Turn.

Armhole shaping: Single crochet in the next 18 (19, 19) stitches, leave the last 4 (5, 6) stitches unworked. Turn. (The skipped stitches form one half of the armhole.)

Next row: Chain 1, single crochet in each stitch across. Turn.

Work even on 18 (19, 19) stitches until there are 43 (43, 45) rows total. Turn.

Neck shaping: Chain 1, single crochet in the next 10 stitches. Leave the last 8 (9, 9) stitches unworked. Turn.

Work even on 10 stitches for 14 (16, 16) more rows until there are 58 (60, 62) rows total. Turn.

Shoulder shaping: Chain 1, single crochet in next 5 stitches, slip stitch in next stitch. End off.

Materials for each size:

- Size: 30" (75 cm) chest measurement
  - 405 yd. (369 m) bulky weight yarn
- Size: 32" (80 cm) chest measurement
  - 460 yd. (419 m) bulky weight yarn
- Size: 34" (85 cm) chest measurement
  - 472 yd. (430 m) bulky weight yarn
- Yarn needle
- Scissors
- Size K/10½ (6.50 mm) crochet hook (I used a hook with a wide throat.)

Skills

- Plain single crochet
- Increase
- Make and use a gauge swatch (See page 103)
- Sew side seams

Gauge

- 11 stitches = 4" (10 cm), 6 rows = 1¾" (4.375 cm)

Ladies finished size:

	Small	Medium	Large
Bust:	30"	32"	34"
	(75 cm)	(80 cm)	(85 cm)
Length:	19"	19"	21"
	(47.5 cm)	(47.5 cm)	(52.5 cm)

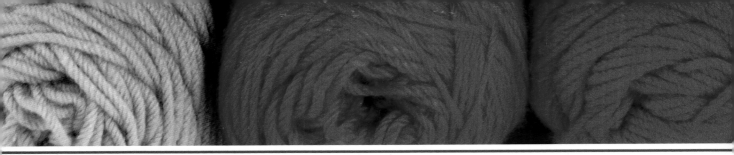

Vest

Right Side Front

(The side that will be on the wearer's right)
Chain 21 (23, 24).

Row 1: Skip 2 chains, single crochet in the third chain from the hook, single crochet in each chain to the last chain, work 2 single crochets in the last chain 20 (22, 23) stitches. Turn.

Row 2: Chain 1, single crochet in each stitch across. Row 2 is worked on the right side. Place a marker on it. Turn.

Row 3: Chain 1, single crochet in each stitch to the last stitch. Work 2 single crochets in the last stitch 21 (23, 24) stitches. Turn.

Row 4: Chain 1, single crochet in each stitch across. Turn.

Row 5: Chain 1, single crochet in each stitch to the last stitch. Work 2 single crochets in the last stitch 22, (24, 25) stitches. Turn.

Work even on 22, (24, 25) stitches until there are 30, (30, 32) rows completed. End off.

Armhole shaping: Turn the piece to the wrong side. With a slip knot on the hook, counting from the right edge of your work, skip 4, (5, 6) stitches. Single crochet in the next 18, (19, 19) stitches. Work even on 18, (19, 19) stitches until there are 43, (43, 45) rows completed. End off.

Neck shaping: Turn the piece so the right side is facing you. With a slip knot on the hook, counting from the right edge, skip 8, (9, 9) stitches. Single crochet in the remaining 10 stitches. Work even on 10 stitches until there are 58, (60, 62) rows completed. End off. Turn to the wrong side.

Shoulder shaping: With a slip knot on the hook, skip 4 stitches. Work a slip stitch in the next stitch. Single crochet in each of the remaining 5 stitches. End off.

The Back

Chain 46, (50, 52).

Row 1: Single crochet in the third chain from the hook and in each chain across 44, (48, 50) stitches. Turn.

Row 2: Chain 1, single crochet in each stitch across. Row 2 is a right-side row. Place a marker on it. Turn.

Work even on 44 (48, 50) stitches until there are 30, (30, 32) rows completed. Fasten off. Turn.

Armhole shaping: With a slip knot on your hook (working on the wrong side) skip 4, (5, 6) stitches. Single crochet in the next stitch. Single crochet to 4, (5, 6) stitches from the end of the row. Leave these 4, (5, 6) stitches unworked 36, (38, 38) stitches. Turn. Work even on 36, (38, 38) stitches until there are 58, (60, 62) rows total. You will end on a right-side row. End off. Turn.

Last row: With a slip knot on your hook, skip 4 stitches. Slip stitch in next single crochet, single crochet in next 5 stitches, slip stitch in the back loop of the next 16, (18, 18) stitches, single crochet in the next 5 stitches, slip stitch in the next stitch, leave the last 4 stitches unworked. End off.

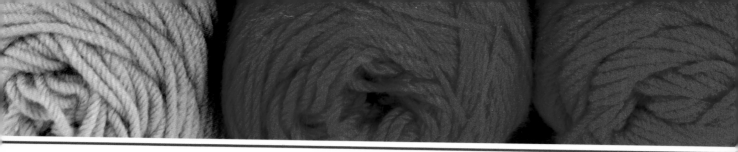

Vest

Sew Your Vest Together

Weave in all the ends. With a length of yarn and a yarn needle, overcast stitch the side of one front piece to the side of the back piece. Make sure the right sides are facing out and match the rows as you sew. Take an extra stitch at the beginning and the end to help secure the stitching. Repeat on the other side. Sew the shoulder seams together, catching the outside loops of the ending row stitches and using an overcast stitch. Weave in all ends.

Ties: Cut 4 pieces of yarn for ties, each 2 yd. (1.82 m) long. Double each of the 4 strands and thread each doubled strand around the top of a stitch on the opening edge of the vest to make 2 facing pairs of ties. The first set of ties should be in the corners and the second set should be 2" (5.0 cm) below the first. Half of each doubled strand will be on either side of the stitch.

For each tie: Twist each half of the doubled strands clockwise, stopping when they are tight to twist around each other in a counter-clockwise direction. Tie an overhand knot in each tie when it is 7" (17.5 cm) long. Trim the ends.

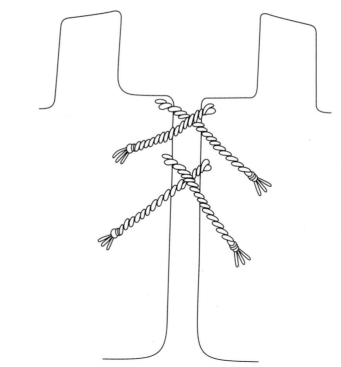

Yarns Used in This Book

Choose any brand of yarn in the same weight and your choice of colors to make the projects as shown. Following are strands of yarn used in the projects in this book. Use this chart, as well as the information given in the instructions, to make your yarn and color selections.

4 by 4's and Hat

TLC Lustre

Lion Brand Cotton Ease

Finger Chains

Lion Brand Wool-Ease Thick & Quick

Lion Brand Landscapes

Lion Brand Chenille Thick & Quick

Lion Brand Glitterspun

Turnover Beanbags

Lion Brand Cotton-Ease

A Yarn Kid

TLC Lustre

A Yarn Kid Scarf and Hat

Lion Brand Wool-Ease

Twisted Potholder

Plymouth Encore

Lion Brand Wool-Ease

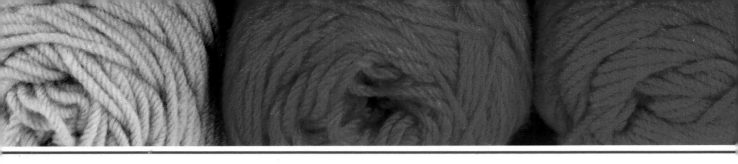

Possibilities Bag

Lily Sugar'n Cream cotton

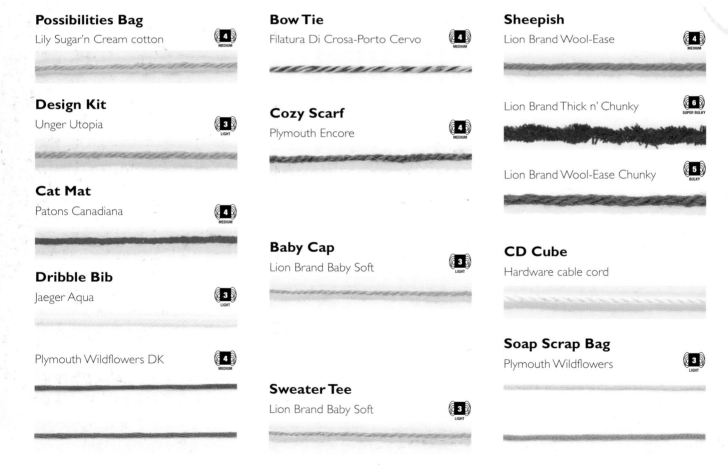

Design Kit

Unger Utopia

Cat Mat

Patons Canadiana

Dribble Bib

Jaeger Aqua

Plymouth Wildflowers DK

Bow Tie

Filatura Di Crosa-Porto Cervo

Cozy Scarf

Plymouth Encore

Baby Cap

Lion Brand Baby Soft

Sweater Tee

Lion Brand Baby Soft

Sheepish

Lion Brand Wool-Ease

Lion Brand Thick n' Chunky

Lion Brand Wool-Ease Chunky

CD Cube

Hardware cable cord

Soap Scrap Bag

Plymouth Wildflowers

Tube Topper
Lion Brand Wool-Ease

Plymouth Encore

A Shining Ornament
DMC #3 Perle Cotton

DMC Metallic Embroidery Floss

Mitten Times Two
Plymouth Encore

Lion Brand Wool-Ease

Tahki Shannon

Knotty Hat
Colorado Yarns Knitaly

Mission Falls

Vest
Lion Brand Wool-Ease Chunky

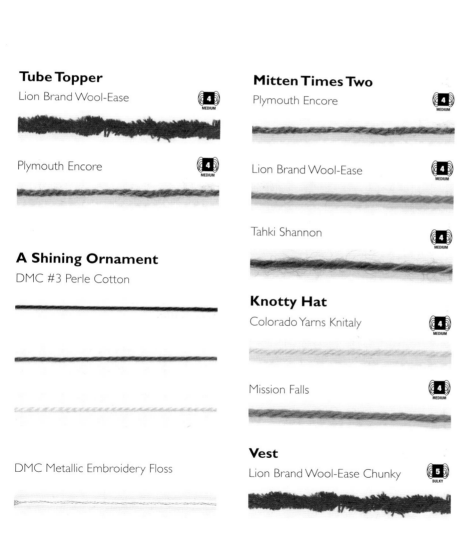

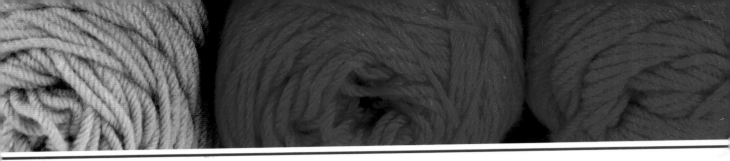

Crochet Abbreviations

Abbreviation	Description
[ ]	work instructions within brackets as many times as directed
( )	work instructions within parentheses as many times as directed
*	repeat the instructions following the single asterisk as directed
* *	repeat instructions between asterisks as many times as directed or repeat from a given set of instructions
"	inch(es)
alt	alternate
approx	approximately
beg	begin/beginning
bet	between
BL	back loop(s)
bo	bobble
BP	back post
BPdc	back post double crochet
BPsc	back post single crochet
BPtr	back post treble crochet
CA	color A
CB	color B
CC	contrasting color
ch	chain stitch

Abbreviation	Description
ch-	refers to chain or space previously made: e.g., ch-1 space
ch-sp	chain spac
CL	cluster
cm	centimeter(s)
cont	continue
dc	double crochet
dc2tog	double crochet 2 stitches together
dec	decrease/decreases/decreasing
dtr	double treble
FL	front loop(s)
foll	follow/follows/following
FP	front post
FPdc	front post double crochet
FPsc	front post single crochet
FPtr	front post treble crochet
g	gram
hdc	half double crochet
inc	increase/increases/increasing
lp(s)	loops
m	meter(s)
MC	main color
mm	millimeter(s)
oz	ounce(s)

Abbreviation	Description
p	picot
pat(s) or patt	pattern(s)
pc	popcorn
pm	place marker
prev	previous
rem	remain/remaining
rep	repeat(s)
rnd(s)	round(s)
RS	right side
sc	single crochet
sc2tog	single crochet 2 stitches together
sk	skip
Sl st	slip sitich
sp(s)	space(s)
st(s)	stitch(es)
tch or t-ch	turning chain
tbl	through back loop
tog	together
tr	treble crochet
trtr	triple treble crochet
WS	wrong side
yd(s)	yard(s)
yo	yarn over
yoh	yarn over hook

UK Crochet Abbreviations

Abbreviation	Description
ch	chain(s)
dc	double crochet (U.K.: tr—treble)
dtr	double treble (U.K.: trtr—triple treble)
grp(s)	group(s)
hdc	half double crochet (U.K.: htr—half treble)
lp(s)	loop(s)
sc	single crochet (U.K.: dc—double crochet)
sl st	slip stitch (U.K.: sc—single crochet)
sp(s)	space(s)
t-ch	turning chain
tr	treble (U.K.: dtr—double treble)
trtr	triple treble (U.K.: qtr—quadruple treble)

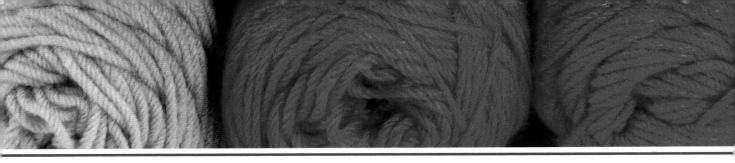

METRIC CONVERSION CHART

Inches to Millimeters and Centimeters

Inches	MM	CM
1/8	3	.3
1/4	6	.6
3/8	10	1.0
1/2	13	1.3
5/8	16	1.6
3/4	19	1.9
7/8	22	2.2
1	25	2.5
1 1/4	32	3.2
1 1/2	38	3.8
1 3/4	44	4.4
2	51	5.1
3	76	7.6
4	102	10.2
5	127	12.7
6	152	15.2
7	178	17.8
8	203	20.3
9	229	22.9
10	254	25.4
11	279	27.9
12	305	30.5

Yards to Meters

Yards	Meters
1/8	.11
1/4	.23
3/8	.34
1/2	.46
5/8	.57
3/4	.69
7/8	.80
1	.91
2	1.83
3	2.74
4	3.66
5	4.57
6	5.47
7	6.40
8	7.32
9	8.23
10	9.14

CROCHET HOOKS

U.S.	METRIC
B/1	2.25 mm
C/2	2.75 mm
D/3	3.25 mm
E/4	3.5 mm
F/5	3.75 mm
G/6	4 mm
7	4.5 mm
H/8	5 mm
I/9	5.5 mm
J/10	6 mm
K/10½	6.5 mm
L/11	8 mm
M/13	9 mm
N/15	10 mm

YARN WEIGHTS

1 SUPER FINE

2 FINE

3 LIGHT

4 MEDIUM

5 BULKY

6 SUPER BULKY

Resources

KP Books
700 E. State St.
Iola, WI 54990-0001
Phone: (800) 258-0929
E-mail: BooksCustomerService@fwpubs.com

Caron International
P.O. Box 222
Washington, NC 27889
www.caron.com

Lion Brand Yarn Company
34 West 15th Street
New York, NY 10011
(212) 243-8995
www.lionbrand.com

Plymouth Yarn Company
P.O. Box 28
Bristol, PA 19007
(215) 788-0459
www.plymouthyarn.com
pyc@plymouthyarn.com

Wm. Wright Company
P.O. Box 398
85 South Street
West Warren, MA 01092-0398
www.ezquilt.com
www.wrights.com
Boye aluminum and steel crochet hooks

Patons Yarn
P.O. Box 40
320 Livingstone Avenue South
Listowel, Ontario Canada
N4H 3H3
(800) 265-2864
www.patonsyarn.com

Lily Cotton
P.O. Box 40
320 Livingstone Avenue South
Listowel, Ontario Canada
N4H 3H3
(800) 265-2864
www.lilyyarns.com

Clover Needlecraft, Inc.
13438 Alondra Boulevard
Cerritos, CA 90703
(800) 233-1703
www.clover-usa.com
Crochet and knitting supplies

Coats & Clark
Consumer Services
P.O. Box 12229
Greenville, SC 29612-0229
(800) 648-1479
www.coatsandclark.com

Patternworks
Route 25
P.O. Box 1618
Center Harbor, NH 03226-1618
(800) 438-5464
www.patternworks.com

Annie's Attic
1 Annie Lane
Big Sandy, TX 75755
800-582-6643
www.anniesattic.com

Herrschners, Inc,
2800 Hoover Rd.
Stevens Point, WI 54481
(800) 441-0838
www.herrschners.com
www.yarnshoppe.com

Tahki-Stacy Charles, Inc.
70-30 80th St. Building 36
Ridgewood, NY 11385
(800) 338 9176
www.tahkistacycharles.com
info@tahkistacycharles.com

Badger Basket Company
P.O. Box 227
Edgar, WI 54426-0227
(800) 236-1310
www.badgerbasket.com
kp@badgerbasket.com
Moses basket

Mary Maxim
2001 Holland Ave
P.O. Box 5019
Port Huron, MI 48061-5019
(800) 962-9504
www.marymaxim.com

Home Sew
P.O. Box 4099
Bethlehem, PA 18018-0099
(800) 344-4739
www.homesew.com

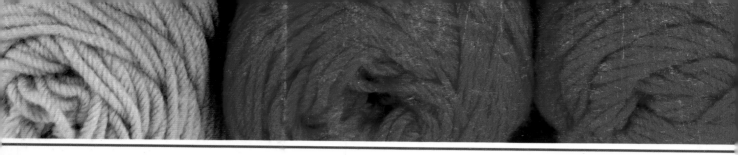

acknowledgments

Many thanks to everyone who helped maké my dream a reality, especially the following:

My husband, Richard, who works at believing personal growth and productivity are more important than a tidy house and home cooked meals.

Ginny Davis, my local yarn store owner, who went beyond her role as yarn supplier to become my personal friend and supporter as I tangle myself ever deeper in the large skein, which is life.

The Knitting Sisters, Cathy, Kat and Carol, the friendly stockers of even more yarn, patience and support at their store, by the same name, in Williamsburg, Virginia.

Mimi Woo, who indulged me by taking time out of her busy schedule at William and Mary college to try on the projects so I could adjust them.

Baby Catherine, my neighbor, who assured me the baby sweater would really fit a 3-month-old child.

Candy Wiza, for her multiple skills as project manager of this book. She not only juggled punctuation and grammar in her editor's role but also acted as "stage manager" for the photography. She kept track of it all with an eye toward "The Opening." I am especially grateful for her accessible, friendly voice whenever I called.

Marilyn McGrane, creative desginer for this book. She enhanced the book with its distinctive style, cover and layout.

Kris Kandler and Robert Best, the photographers, who were the human eyes behind the camera's eye.

Melinda Bylow and Emily Adler, for all of their wonderful and creative illustrations.

Meagan Button and Shelby Richter, for modeling the projects. You both have great smiles and a natural manner in front of the camera.

Lillian Gliszinski, Sarah Richter and Shelby Richter (a true generational family) for reminding all of us that crochet can be a great family pastime to share.

Karen Klemp, past president of The Crochet Guild of America and crochet instructor at Aylin's Woolgatherer in Falls Church, Virginia. Karen is a calm, knowledgeable and reassuring voice, even as she pursues her own creative adventures.